"Ben Shaw does not write this book from some theological ivory tower. He writes as a man in the midst of a life-threatening battle with cancer. I found that that fact gave every chapter such a ring of authenticity. This book is clear, well-argued, compelling, vivid and personal. I thoroughly commend it."

RICO TICE, Senior Minister (Evangelism), All Soul's Church, London, UK; Founder, Christianity Explored Ministries

"A very personal and personable case for the open-minded to consider or reconsider the claims of Christ. It's easy to pick up and hard to put down. Enjoy the challenge to think again."

PHILLIP JENSEN, Founder, Two Ways to Live Ministries

"I enjoyed this book and would highly recommend it to anyone wanting to investigate Christianity. Ben writes with honesty and humour as he sets out why the Christian faith is intellectually credible, great news and worthy of serious consideration."

ADRIAN BLIGHT, Consultant Physician, London

"What a great book to put into the hands of a person who has either never really considered Christianity or who has lost their way. I kept on thinking of people for whom the clarity and simplicity of the engaging presentation might just be what it takes to challenge their misconceptions."

MARK CALDER, Anglican Bishop, Diocese of Bathurst, NSW, Australia

"What a great book. Ben doesn't duck any thorny issues that people might have with the Bible, but tackles them head on, with refreshing honesty, humility and skill. True to Ben's Australian roots, *7 reasons to (re)consider Christianity* is a relaxed read, and his anecdotes entertain; you could definitely read this book at the beach or with a beer in hand!"

SARAH HALL, Women's Worker, Emmanuel Church, Wimbledon, UK

"If you want to take a first, second or hundredth look at Christianity, then this book is for you."

GAVIN SHUME, Executive Director, Matthias Media Australia

BEN SHAW

7 reasons to (re)consider Christianity

Seven Reasons to (Re)Consider Christianity
© Ben Shaw, 2021. Reprinted 2021.

Published by:
The Good Book Company

thegoodbook.com | thegoodbook.co.uk
thegoodbook.com.au | thegoodbook.co.nz | thegoodbook.co.in

ISBN: 9781784986346 | Printed in the UK

Design by André Parker

Contents

Introduction   7

1. Because it's worth thinking
   through what life is really all about   11

2. Because Christianity is a lot
   more intellectually credible than
   you might have assumed   25

3. Because Christianity is about
   life to the full   45

4. Because Christianity gives a compelling
   answer to the question "What's wrong
   with the world?"   63

5. Because Jesus is arguably the most
   influential person in history   79

6. Because the death of Jesus is
   surprisingly very good news for you   97

7. Because, if Jesus really did rise
   from the dead, then it would
   confirm everything   111

P.S. Why I've (re)considered Christianity   133

What next?   137

Acknowledgements and Endnotes   139

To my father

Introduction

I don't know how you have ended up holding this book in your hands, but whatever the reason, it was written for you: the inquirer, the curious, the inquisitive, the sceptic, the atheist, the agnostic, and even the doubting Christian. Whoever you are, I'm glad you're here.

I realise that for some of you it might have been a while since you had anything to do with Christianity. It's been ages since you've stepped into a church or glanced at a Bible. Perhaps you went to church as a kid, but you've never really looked at the Christian faith as an adult. But now, for one reason or another, you're wondering whether it's time to look at it afresh and reconsider Christianity.

Or perhaps, like me, you grew up in a family that wasn't religious at all. Christianity has never been on your radar. You're either an atheist or an agnostic, but you don't go to church and have never really believed in God. You've never looked seriously at the Bible or studied the life of Jesus, and besides, all those stories and commands just seem irrelevant to you—and frankly, not very believable. Or maybe you've always suspected that there is a "god" of some kind out there, but you're not sure what or who. Or perhaps you're of another faith altogether, but now you're curious as to whether there's something worth considering about Christianity.

So, whether you're reconsidering Christianity or considering Christianity for the first time, I hope you keep reading.

Of course, you might have any number of different personal reasons for reading this book. Perhaps you're willing to read it because something has happened in your life that has aroused a renewed interest in regards to faith. Or you might have been inspired by a thought-provoking Christian friend.

As a church minister I regularly run introductory courses on Christianity, and people come for a whole lot of reasons. They may be prompted by the death of a friend or family member, a deep conversation they had over a glass of wine about the meaning of life, a discussion about the reliability of the Bible over a coffee, a talk or sermon they heard recently, or a movie or documentary they watched. It may be that they have met an admirable Christian or had a positive experience at a church or their kids have begun to ask them questions about religion, God, faith and so on.

Personally speaking, I first began to think about God and the Bible for several reasons combined: the death of my mother, the question of the meaning of life, a curiosity about the stories of Jesus and a desire to know what happens when we die.

That journey began over four decades ago. My life has taken many twists and turns since then, but through it all, my faith in Jesus has brought me more hope and joy and meaning than I could ever have imagined.

I hope you'll read this book cover to cover, but I suspect one or two chapters will hit a personal sweet spot. Feel free to jump straight to those chapters if you want to. I don't expect that this book alone will necessarily "convert" you, but I do hope that it at least helps you see the intellectual credibility of the Christian's position, shows you why it's good news, and sets you on a journey to find out more.

In the end, I really hope it makes you think and (re)consider Christianity for yourself.

1. Because it's worth thinking through what life is really all about

"For as long as I can remember, I've been searching for some reason why we're here—what are we doing here, who are we? If this is a chance to find out even just a little part of that answer, I think it's worth a human life, don't you?"

Dr Ellie Arroway, played by Jodie Foster in the film *Contact*

Several years ago, Bolton Wanderers were playing Tottenham Hotspur in a Football Association Cup quarter final in London. During the first half of the match, one of the Bolton players, Fabrice Muamba, suddenly collapsed in the middle of the pitch. At first no one knew why the 23-year-old had suddenly crumpled to the ground. He was nowhere near the ball at the time, but pretty soon every player around him could see he was in deep trouble. The players motioned to the medics, who promptly ran onto the field. It became apparent that Muamba was having a heart attack. A deafening silence came over the whole stadium.

Thankfully, one of the spectators in the crowd was Andrew Deaner, a consultant cardiologist at the London Chest Hospital. He immediately sensed what was happening and instinctively ran onto the field to help. More than 30,000 spectators watched these dedicated doctors pump on this young man's heart as he lay in the middle of a stadium on the brink of death.

It was incredibly moving to hear two sets of fans within the stadium become one, going from long spells of silence to applauding together as they tried to encourage the medics and will Fabrice on. His heart was still being worked on as he was stretchered from the ground into a waiting ambulance. Understandably, the game was immediately abandoned. This, by the way, was all happening while his wife and three-year-old son were watching the game at home on TV.

The story has a happy ending though. Fabrice Muamba survived and, after a suspenseful few days in hospital, made a full recovery, despite his heart stopping for an incredible 78 minutes! Yet everyone watching in that stadium—and reading the headlines subsequently—was left with a sobering reminder: none of us are immune to death. It can strike anyone of us at any time, even in the prime of our lives.

STOP AND THINK

It's often only when we're fully confronted by death that we really think about the meaning of life. Death or near-death experiences often lead us to ask ourselves big questions like: What if that was me? What happens when we die? What's life really all about? Is there a God?

I once came across a grave that had these words inscribed on the tombstone:

"Passer-by, stop and think:
I'm in eternity; you are on the brink!"

If we're all on the edge of eternity, in the words of that tombstone we ought to stop and think—don't you think?! That is, we should all consider what life is all about, not just when we're confronted by death but far more frequently.

However, it often seems that thinking about the meaning of life is a dying art these days. Those who stop to think about the meaning of life are an endangered species in our culture. That is perhaps because we have so many different things crying out for our attention and consuming our valuable time, be it our phones, Netflix, emails, shopping, cooking, kids, music, social media, exercising, holidays, cleaning, renovations, finances, jobs and so on.

So pause here and ask yourself these questions:

- What do you think the meaning or purpose of life is?

- Why are we all here?

- Are we all here by chance—the result of some freak cosmic accident that happened billions of years ago?

- Are we just a collection of random atoms that have simply evolved over time?

- Or is there a purpose behind it all: a grand plan to the universe?

- Is there a God or something like that which suggests there's more to life than meets the eye?

- And what happens when we die? Are we just food for worms or is there another dimension beyond the grave?

Whatever your answers might be, these are questions that are at least worth thinking about.

SEARCHING THE UNIVERSE FOR UNIVERSAL ANSWERS

Humankind has always searched for meaning and purpose. You see this in the writings of ancient Greek philosophers and in the sacred texts of all the major religions. You can detect it in the greatest novels and essays ever penned.

Even many of our scientific endeavours, both ancient and modern, have their origins in trying to understand our significance in the universe or control our destiny in life. We're trying to find out what's over there, up there, under there, around there or just out there.

I'm totally captivated by space exploration. My inner geek comes out whenever the next NASA or SpaceX rocket takes off. Space exploration is not just driven by the desire to boldly go where no one has gone before but by the desire to find answers to our biggest and deepest questions.

Bruce Jakosky is a planetary scientist and the director of a team within the NASA Astrobiology Institute—to date, he's been involved in every one of NASA's missions to Mars. When it comes to justifying NASA's motives for space exploration, he has said this:

"We're interested in the search for extrasolar planets because it tells us ... is our solar system unique or common? ... We are interested in the possibility of life on Mars because it provides context for understanding the value of life on Earth ... By learning about the worlds around us, we are learning about ourselves."[1]

This same sentiment is central to one of my favourite films of the 1990s, *Contact*, based on a book of the same name by the astrophysicist Carl Sagan. It's been called "the movie that asks the big questions". Jodie Foster plays Dr Ellie Arroway, a scientist who is searching for extra-terrestrial life by listening to pulses through radio telescopes. At a pivotal point in the film she pauses to say these lines, with which we began this chapter, to her questioning co-star:

"For as long as I can remember, I've been searching for some reason why we're here—what are we doing here, who are we? If this is a chance to find out even just a little part of that answer, I think it's worth a human life, don't you?"

I totally relate to that burning desire for answers. Sometimes I wonder whether, for me, it stems from the death of my mother when I was seven years old. Or does it come from camping trips with my friends, when we slept under the stars, stared into space and talked about the possibility of life elsewhere in the universe? Maybe in part. But actually, I don't think the desire for answers is unique to me. It lies deep within every human heart.

THE LONGING IN EVERY HUMAN HEART

Alongside the questions and ambitions of our philosophers and rocket scientists, perhaps the quest for meaning and purpose is no more evident than within the lyrics and poems of our musicians and poets.

I'm showing my age now, but I was, and still am, a fan of the singer-songwriter John Mellencamp. You might know him from songs like "Jack & Diane", "Pink Houses" or "Hurts So Good". Many years ago now, he penned a very honest song entitled "Void in My Heart". It's definitely worth a listen.

Here was a rock star at the height of his career, in bare honesty, revealing his deepest longings and how his life of fame and fortune just wasn't doing it for him. Maybe you know how that feels. Like John Mellencamp, we can reach the pinnacle of our profession and amass great wealth yet still have an overwhelming sense of emptiness and longing.

Mellencamp's lyrics actually echo part of an old poem written by Solomon, king of ancient Israel around 3,000 years ago. It's preserved for us in the Old Testament part of the Bible:

I said to myself, "Come now, I will test you with pleasure to find out what is good." But that also proved to be meaningless. "Laughter," I said, "is madness. And what does pleasure accomplish?" I tried cheering myself with wine, and embracing folly—my mind still guiding me with wisdom. I wanted to see what was good for people to do under the heavens during the few days of their lives.

I undertook great projects: I built houses for myself and planted vineyards. I made gardens and parks and planted all kinds of fruit trees in them. I made reservoirs to water groves of flourishing trees. I bought male and female slaves and had other slaves who were born in my house. I also owned more herds and flocks than anyone in Jerusalem before me. I amassed silver and gold for myself, and the treasure of kings and provinces. I acquired male and female singers, and a harem as well—the delights of a man's heart. I became greater by far than anyone in Jerusalem before me.

In all this my wisdom stayed with me. I denied myself nothing my eyes desired; I refused my heart no pleasure. My heart took delight in all my labour, and this was the reward for all my toil. Yet when I surveyed all that my hands had done and what I had toiled to achieve, everything was meaningless, a chasing after the wind; nothing was gained under the sun. (Ecclesiastes, chapter 2, verses 1-11)

Can you relate to these words of Solomon? Even after three millennia, there's a strikingly modern ring to them. We go to work, we socialise with our friends, we sometimes reach our ambitions, we have our holidays, and most of us (in the West) have all the toys we could ever need—yet so many of us are still unsatisfied and looking for more.

Sure, we may be fairly happy and content, and have a reasonable sense of fulfilment; I wouldn't claim otherwise. Most of my friends who aren't religious, including members of my own family, would say they're *reasonably* happy and content. But most of us still feel that there's something more to life than just what meets the eye— that there's more to our existence than just living for 80 years or so and then dying. John Mellencamp felt it, King Solomon felt it and I'm guessing you have felt it too. There seems to be a timeless and universal sense that there's something else going on.

THE MAN WITH THE ANSWERS

In the 1st century, around 2,000 years ago, Jesus made some astonishing claims and gave the world some mind-bending answers to our deepest questions about life and why we're all here. With great confidence, he talked about the meaning of life, true love, the reality and nature of God, where to find hope and happiness, and what happens to us beyond the grave. He taught his followers about "life … to the full" and how to get it (John 10 v 10). He effectively gave the greatest series of TED Talks of all time, holding audiences captivated for hours on end. Jesus gave answers to many of the questions that we humans have been asking ourselves since the beginning of time.

You may not have given Christianity any serious thought as an adult or even as a child, but here are two reasons why Jesus and his teachings about life are worth considering.

First, while there have been many people who have given their answers to life's biggest questions, none have had a worldwide impact as much as Jesus. (I'll say a lot more about this in chapter 5.) He is arguably the most influential person that has ever lived. He has inspired art and architecture for centuries. More songs and books have been written about him than about any other figure in history. Apparently, the Library of Congress in Washington, D.C. is regarded as the largest library on the planet. A librarian with a little too much time on their hands has calculated that this library has more than 800 miles of shelving containing more than 24 million catalogued books in over 400 languages. But out of all those millions of volumes, there are, by far, more books on Jesus than on any other person that's ever lived—over 17,000 of them.[2]

What Jesus has said seems to have struck a chord with many of us. And even if you disagree with what he had to say, his answers are at least worth taking an honest and open-minded look at from a cultural and educational point of view.

Second, Jesus backed up his words with incredible actions. He wasn't just an amazing orator or wordsmith with some fancy answers to our deepest questions. When he talked about life and life to the full, he backed it up by raising people from the dead. When he talked about seeing what the world was really all about, he then healed people from blindness. And when he preached about love and servant-heartedness being the keys to living a fulfilled life, he then went on to serve others and give up his own life to a grisly death on a Roman cross. If you're sceptical about whether all that is really possible, that's fair enough—please read on to chapter 5. But for now, consider that if these actions of Jesus were even *half* true and he really was who he claimed to be, then what he had to say about life deserves our attention.

Christianity offers some profound and honest answers to our deepest questions and longings, backed up by the incredible life of the person as its centre: Jesus Christ. Through his words, parables and teachings, he gave powerful and thought-provoking answers to the very questions so many of us innately have; and those answers have actually shaped our world. Surely they are at least worth considering, aren't they?

WHAT IF IT'S TRUE?

I once heard a story about two men who were walking along a beach in the Florida Keys, U.S.A. The two were happily soaking up the tranquillity of the seaside as they meandered for a mile or so along the shoreline, when one of them spotted a bottle washed up onto the sand. On closer inspection, they saw that the bottle contained documents wrapped neatly in an official-looking ribbon.

They opened the bottle and pulled out a legal will for a personal estate.

In disbelief, they read the contents of the opening letter on the first page: "Whoever finds this bottle and the contents within is entitled to inherit my whole estate". The bottle contained more official documents and the contact details of a solicitor who would verify that the whole thing was authentic.

The two men had vastly different opinions as to what to do next. One of them said, "Ah what a crock! It's surely a hoax. It's too good to be true. Throw it back into the sea for someone more gullible. Let's go!" and promptly walked off. The other guy called after him, "Yeah, but what if it is true? What if this is real? Isn't it at least worth investigating? Maybe it is a hoax; maybe it's not. But, as the stakes are so high and we have little to lose, shouldn't we at least consider it?" At which he folded up the papers and put them in his pocket, and ran after his friend.

A few days later, the man with the documents rang the phone number given in the letter. It turned out that the whole thing was true. And after several weeks of investigations and legal work, he eventually ended up inheriting over $5million worth of cash and real estate.

I'm asking you to (re)consider Christianity on the basis of the same question: What if it's all true? What if Jesus really was who he claimed to be, and he did have the answers to our biggest questions? I know it's hard to believe, and there are many reasons we may have for not investigating, but what if this Jesus fella really does have the answers to what we're all ultimately looking for? What if there really is a God, and there is such a thing as eternal life beyond the grave? That would be worth far more than $5million dollars. Imagine how much purpose, peace and joy that would infuse into your life. That would be priceless.

A Christian friend of mine had a neighbour who had never really looked into the Christian faith beyond his early years of school. From time to time she would casually chat with him about God and the meaning of life and so on, until one day she plucked up the courage to invite him to church. To her surprise, he gladly accepted. She picked a particular Sunday when she knew a gifted preacher was coming to her church for an event aimed at non-religious people. This preacher was an excellent communicator who had spoken at churches all over the world, and a bestselling author to boot. He seemed the ideal person to introduce her neighbour to Christianity.

On the given Sunday, she drove her neighbour to church full of eager expectation and excitement. They arrived at the church only to find out that she had got the date wrong. The guest preacher was due the following Sunday, not this one! Worse still, the regular minister was away on holiday, and so an older member of the church was filling in.

Her heart sank. She had heard this guy speak once before, and he wasn't a great preacher at all. To make matters even worse, the Bible passage he was going to speak on was what's called a genealogy—a long list of names specifying how many years each person had lived for. Basically the passage went something like this: *So and so begat so and so. He lived for this many years, and then he died. Then his son begat so and so, and he lived for this many years, and then he died. Then his son begat so and so, and he lived for this many years, and then he died,* and so on and so on.

After the Bible passage was read, this man got up and preached on it for a whole 45 minutes. The congregation were bored senseless, with half of them asleep in the pews by the end of the sermon.

As the service concluded, this woman turned to her friend and apologised profusely for getting him out of bed early on a Sunday morning only to end up enduring such a boring sermon. She then promptly drove this poor guy home expecting him never to return to church again.

However, the whole experience had an unexpected and profound effect on him. As he went to bed that night, he couldn't sleep—he couldn't stop thinking about that long genealogy. The words *and then he died, and then he died, and then he died* kept ringing round his head. He'd never really thought about his death very much before and therefore hadn't given much thought to what life was really all about. So he ended up going back to the church to find out more. After months of discussions and questions, he began to investigate the words and life of Jesus for himself, and eventually he came to the conclusion that it was all true and worth committing to.

So what about you? Have you thought about your death lately—or about life, and what it's all about? And what do you make of this man who has had such a huge impact on world history? Do you know enough to have an informed opinion?

As I see it, Christianity is at least worth thinking about because it is offering us some incredible, thought-provoking answers to our biggest and deepest questions, from the most influential person in history. You may find that you do not agree with what Jesus taught, and you may not come to the same conclusion as my friend's neighbour—but isn't the meaning of your existence at least worth thinking about? Even if you come to a different conclusion, at least consider what Christianity is all about. Don't throw the bottle back in the water. Open it and see.

2. Because Christianity is a lot more intellectually credible than you might have assumed

Interviewer: "You accept the historical existence of Jesus?"
Albert Einstein: "Unquestionably! No one can read the Gospels
without feeling the actual presence of Jesus. His personality
pulsates in every word. No myth is filled with such life."

Interview by George Sylvester Viereck with Albert Einstein, as recorded in
Einstein: His life and Universe by Walter Isaacson, p 386

I have a lot of sympathy when it comes to the questions and doubts of my sceptical and atheist friends. I really do get it. I understand their reservations about the stories of the Bible and the Christian faith. I had them too once.

So, even now that I'm a committed Christian, I want to be honest and concede that I do believe some things that may sound pretty strange to you. I believe that 2,000 years ago God literally became a human being, who was born of a virgin in a tiny little backward town named Bethlehem. I believe that Jesus could bend nature: that he calmed a storm, walked on a Galilean lake and turned water into wine. I believe that he healed the sick and cured the lame. I believe that he died on a Roman cross for the sins of the world and, perhaps most impressive of all, rose from the dead a few days later. As a Christian, I also believe that the Bible is the inspired word of God, that he really is listening to our prayers and that he's in control of the world, despite what sometimes seems like evidence to the contrary.

All that, if I'm honest, can sound pretty weird and counter-intuitive to a rational, scientific, 21st-century mind.

So, at one level, it's no surprise to me that Christians are therefore sometimes labelled as gullible, ignorant or stupid. I've been called all those things, and worse! Lots of people assume that believing in God and the Christian story is akin to believing in Santa Claus or fairies at the bottom of the garden; and that Christians are just intellectual infants.

But in this chapter, I'm asking you to reconsider that, for a number of reasons.

THERE ARE MANY CHRISTIANS WHO ARE INTELLECTUALS

First of all, the Christian church is, and has always been, full of intellectuals—academics and scholars who have weighed up the arguments, looked long and hard at the evidence, and found that their faith in a miraculous man from Galilee in Israel is both rational and intellectually sustainable. In fact, some of the smartest people who have ever lived have had a faith in God and taken the Bible seriously: Origen, Augustine, Hildegard of Bingen, Thomas Aquinas, Thomas Cranmer, Martin Luther, James David Forbes, Lord Kelvin, Mary Anning, Leo Tolstoy, Karl Barth, Dorothy L. Sayers, C. S. Lewis, Søren Kierkegaard, Os Guinness, John Lennox, Alvin C. Plantinga, Lynn Cohick, N.T. Wright, William Lane Craig, Alister McGrath, Rosalind Picard, Jennifer Wiseman and Katharine Hayhoe, just to name a few. You may have to Google a few of those names, but you'll find that they all had, or still have, brains the size of a small country.

In fact, of the 500 or so Nobel Prize recipients of the 20th century, over 65% have identified themselves as Christians. I personally know Christians who are solicitors, brain surgeons, historians, judges, archaeologists, chemists, mathematicians, philosophy lecturers and professors. None of them take their beliefs lightly or suspend their intellect to accommodate their faith. They are men and women who have good, intelligent reasons for believing in God and taking the Bible seriously. To dismiss all Christians as naive or gullible or infantile in their thinking is unfair and simply doesn't reflect the truth.

THE RATIONALITY OF BELIEVING IN GOD

Second, there is a good case for the existence of God to be made from what appears to be intelligent design in nature. Whether Christian or not, the majority of people in the world today believe that there is *someone* or at least *something* behind the cosmos in which we all find ourselves (the secular West is actually in the minority). The very word "cosmos" is an ancient Greek word that literally means "orderly beauty". (That's also how we get the word "cosmetics".)

We seem to live in a world that is characterised by intentional beauty, design and order. For many of us, it's reasonably logical to assume that there is some kind of grand intelligence behind this world. As a friend of mine used to say, "There seem to be divine fingerprints everywhere we look".

In fact, it could be said that it's *disbelief* in a Creator that is actually intellectually unsustainable. If we remove God from the equation of life, then we get a philosophical domino effect that leads to some serious consequences. At the very least, it makes many of life's big questions very hard to answer. Are human beings inherently valuable? On what basis? Where do we ground our morality as a society? What makes one thing right and another thing wrong, and why? What are human beings here for? If we really are all here simply because of some accidental cosmic burp billions of years ago, then we're just advanced amoebas, roaming around on a lonely planetary rock, with no ultimate purpose and no final hope for living. We really are just food for worms when we die, and if that's the case, we should just crack on with that age-old, hedonistic philosophy that says, "Eat, drink and be merry, for tomorrow we die!"

THE HISTORICITY OF THE BIBLE

Third, and the main argument of this chapter, there is actually a lot of good evidence for the historicity and reliability of the Bible, especially the four Gospels (the biographies of Jesus called Matthew, Mark, Luke and John).

I know that many people think otherwise. Or maybe you're reading this as someone who might be willing to investigate the existence of God, but you still find it hard to believe that the Bible is a trustworthy starting point. Hasn't the Bible changed over the centuries? Can a rational, thinking person really believe in all those science-suspending miracles? Is there any credible historical proof for all those incredible stories? Again, these are fair and understandable questions. If Christians claim that their whole faith in God hinges on a historical figure from a real place in the Middle East, and that the stories about him in the Bible are historical events, an intelligent person is going to ask probing questions about the evidence.

A few years ago, I was in my local London pub, writing a talk on this very topic, when a group of about twelve people came in and sat at a large table next to me. I couldn't help eavesdropping on their conversation, trying to ascertain who they were. They seemed like a friendly bunch, so, in a moment of rare boldness, I turned and asked them, "Do you mind if I ask you all a question?" With a look of curiosity, they all happily agreed, and I began to tell them that I was a preacher and was writing a talk on the historical reliability of the New Testament. I then fired my question: *If you could pinpoint one thing above all others, what is it that stops you believing in God and the Bible?*

The overwhelming response of just about all of them was "Not enough evidence". Turns out they were a group of senior and junior detectives from a local police academy. As I chatted with them, one of them said to me, "Our jobs are all about evidence, and I've never been convinced there's enough evidence when it comes to the Bible". I asked him if he had ever seriously looked at the Bible and the evidence for it for himself, and he sheepishly confessed with a smile that he actually hadn't.

He's not the only person to dismiss the Bible with sweeping assessments that there's "not enough evidence" but with no real basis for those conclusions. So many people I've come across write off the Bible on extremely thin arguments.

Let me suggest two reasons why you might want to reconsider the historical reliability of the Bible.

ALL ANCIENT HISTORY IS RIDDLED WITH GAPS

First of all, to say that there's not enough evidence that the stories in the Bible actually happened is a little unfair. If you applied that same degree of historical assessment to other events in history, you'd have to wipe out virtually everything and everyone we know from the ancient world.

Cleopatra VII, the queen of Egypt and lover of Mark Antony, is arguably the most famous female of antiquity, yet we have no tomb or mummified body of her. What we know of her mainly comes from written sources, just like those in the Bible, but no one questions her existence or the generally accepted facts about her life.

Or take the Battle of Actium, which took place on the western coast of Greece in 31 BC—one of the most famous naval battles of the Roman Empire. You can read much about it from a number of different ancient accounts, yet we have no hard proof that this battle ever occurred other than our written sources. According to one account (Plutarch's *Life of Antony*, 68:1), around 700 ships were involved, with more than 5,000 casualties. (That's more than double the number of Pearl Harbor during World War Two.) Many of the ships were sunk, some very close to the coast of mainland Western Greece, yet we have not found a single shipwreck to prove that the battle took place. Despite several expeditions, marine archaeologists today still haven't uncovered any convincing archaeological proof that this battle actually happened. But again, as far as I know, there are no scholars saying that the Battle of Actium therefore never happened.

Fast forward over 1,500 years later to one of England's most famous sons: William Shakespeare. Despite a plethora of historians delving into his past, we still don't know when this giant of English literature was born! We can take an educated guess at it on account of a baptismal entry in his local church, but we don't know his actual birthday. Likewise, the birth date of Christopher Columbus, Anne Boleyn (the second wife of King Henry VIII), Ludwig van Beethoven, Daniel Boone and Jack Daniel (of Tennessee Whiskey fame) are all unknown to us. (And as far as Jack Daniel goes, other than the year, we don't know the date of his death either!)

The point is, much of history is full of evidential blanks, and historians have always had to do a fair amount of joining the dots and filling in the gaps for *almost any event or person from history*. The fact is that just about all ancient history struggles when it comes to solid confirmation through watertight evidence.

Also, keep in mind that the further we go back in time, the less evidence there is for historical events. We still don't know exactly how the pyramids were built or where exactly King Nebuchadnezzar's famous Hanging Gardens of Babylon once stood. Both of these things that I've just mentioned belong to that famous club "The Seven Wonders of the Ancient World" and yet they're still shrouded in mystery.

It should come as no surprise, then, that some of the Bible's most famous stories—such as those of Moses and the Israelites' escape from slavery in Egypt, and the journey to the promised land, recorded in the book of Exodus—have no other external evidence to back them up. But concluding (as some critics do) that these things therefore never happened is a little unreasonable, given how long ago the exodus took place. All historians will tell you that just about any event dating from that far back (around 1250 BC) is unlikely to be verified by lots of solid evidence. Plus, what trace would you expect to find of a bunch of nomadic, ex-slaves in a sand-blown desert over 3,000 years later? Furthermore, there's no way that the great, proud Egyptians would have recorded the humiliating loss of thousands of slaves in their own hieroglyphic inscriptions—indeed, it's likely they'd have wanted to deliberately airbrush out such an event. It therefore comes as no surprise that we have no equivalent Egyptian record to the biblical account of the exodus.

THERE'S PLENTY OF EVIDENCE FOR MUCH OF THE BIBLE

But when it comes to other events of the Bible, it's not true to say there's little evidence. There are tons of it... literally! I regularly run private tours of the British Museum in London on biblically related artefacts, and, once a year, I have the privilege of guiding around 35 adults on archaeological tours of Israel. It's very easy for people to see first-hand the overwhelming amount of evidence that confirms much of the Bible.

Again, you may need to google some of these, but artefacts such the Assyrian Black Obelisk of Shalmaneser III, the Cyrus Cylinder, the Taylor Prism, the Lachish Stone Reliefs, the inscription on the Tel Dan Stele, the Silver Amulets, the Pilate Stone unearthed in Caesarea, the

Caiaphas Ossuary, and remains from the Pool of Siloam and the Temple Mount (just to name a few) all in some ways help authenticate the biblical accounts which they're related to.

Again, particularly when it comes to the New Testament (the section of the Bible written after Jesus' life on earth), in many cases there's far *more* evidence for these documents than there are for many other events of antiquity that we take for granted. It's simply not true, and frankly, quite ignorant, to say there's little historical proof for the stories about Jesus.

What is historically compelling about the New Testament accounts about Jesus of Nazareth? Here are some things worth considering.

1. The academic consensus is that Jesus existed as a historical person

In the UK, one the fastest-growing myths (alongside the flat-earth theory) is that Jesus never existed. However, in all my years of research I haven't found a single accredited historian *in this field of ancient history* who has ever really maintained a serious denial that Jesus was a historical figure. Yes, since the Enlightenment of the 18th century there have been a few people who have flirted with the theory, but most books questioning the existence of Jesus are, at best, written by pseudo-scholars who have never published their works in peer-reviewed journals of ancient history.

In his book *The God Delusion*, atheist Richard Dawkins doesn't fully deny that Jesus existed, but he does suggest there's a possibility that he didn't exist. However, to back up the questionability of Jesus' historical existence, the only scholar he manages to muster by name is G. A. Wells, who wrote a book or two on the topic.[3] What Dawkins doesn't tell you is that Wells was a professor of German literature, not of ancient history, and that sometime later he in fact recanted some of his theory and conceded that Jesus did most likely exist.[4]

A few years ago, a very good friend of mine who himself holds a PhD in a particular field of 1st-century Greco-Roman history, got in contact with three eminent ancient historians and asked them if they knew of any credible historian that firmly held the view that Jesus didn't exist. All three of them said no. And one of them, Professor Graham Clarke of the Australian National University (who is not a Christian), emailed back to my friend with these words: "Frankly I know of no ancient historian or biblical historian that would have a twinge of doubt about the existence of Jesus Christ. The documentary evidence is simply overwhelming ... and you can quote me." (So I am!)

2. There are lots of sources

The Bible isn't simply one source written by one individual. Rather, the Bible is a collection of multiple documents (letters, biographies, narrative history, poems, songs and more) written by dozens of different people, living in a whole range of situations, over a long period of time. So in the New Testament, we don't just have one or two documents on Jesus and the early Christians written by one or two authors, but 27 documents written by eight or nine different authors.

Added to this, Jesus and the first generation of his followers are referred to multiple times in other ancient literature outside the Bible. Jesus is mentioned, at least in passing, in as many as ten to twelve different 1st- and 2nd-century Jewish and Roman documents that we have from the period. In fact, from these non-Christian documents alone, we can still work out where Jesus lived, when Jesus lived, that he taught many people, that he did miracles (or at least that he did things that were thought to be miraculous), that he had a devoted band of followers, that he was called "the Christ", that he was tried by the Roman governor Pontius Pilate, that he was crucified in Jerusalem and that many people claimed that he rose from the dead. We can glean all of that from ancient sources without opening a Bible or turning to the scores of other documents written by early Christians.

3. The Bible is specific (and therefore verifiable)

On many occasions the Bible writers describe specific buildings, towns, villages and geographical landscapes in considerable detail that can easily be verified, even 2,000 years later. They reference religious leaders, governors, kings, emperors and philosophers of the day. They give us distances, dates and, in some cases, even the time of day when a certain event happened. And they name specific eyewitnesses to the events they record.

Take one of the opening sentences in Luke's Gospel, for example. Luke tells us that the birth of Jesus happened:

> *In the time of Herod king of Judea there was a priest named Zechariah, who belonged to the priestly division of Abijah; his wife Elizabeth was also a descendant of Aaron.*
>
> *(Luke 1 v 5)*

He doesn't say, "A long, long time ago in a galaxy far, far away..." He gives us five testable names, a geographical location and a couple of job titles (king, priest). Details like these leave the Bible well and truly wide open to historical verification, both then and now. While we can't verify *everything* in the Bible, in the overwhelming majority of cases, the other historical accounts and archaeological evidence that we have does match up with Scripture.

Admittedly, on a couple of occasions (as with any hundreds of other ancient documents), the biblical accounts don't always square with other accounts that we have from the same period. Two common examples are taken from the second chapter of Luke: "In those days Caesar Augustus issued a decree that a census should be taken of the entire Roman world. (This was the first census that took place while Quirinius was governor of Syria.)" (Luke 2 v 1-5). To date we have no corroborating evidence of a census of this scale in the 1st century, and, according to other sources, Quirinius didn't become the governor of Syria until about ten years after the death of Herod the Great (who is significant in Matthew's account of Jesus' birth). Some suggest that Luke got his facts wrong; others claim that Luke deliberately fudged the story to suit his own agenda. Either way, the suggestion is that we therefore can't trust the Bible, or Luke's Gospel at least.

Some of my sceptical friends have been quick to point out to me these apparent inconsistencies on several occasions, but a more level-headed approach, given our limited sources, is to think through a couple of scenarios that could square the conflicting accounts. It is possible that two different men named Quirinius were governor of Syria, or, more likely, that Quirinius had two terms of office. Or perhaps we're simply missing a few pieces of the puzzle that explain the differences in the accounts.

In regards to the census, we also know that Roman emperors did order numerous head counts for taxation purposes in various regions of the empire on several occasions. In fact, Augustus ordered at least three censuses in the period in question.[5]

What a lot of people fail to account for is that whenever we get two, three or more different accounts about any event in ancient history (or modern history for that matter), they almost never align completely. The fact that one account in the New Testament doesn't line up exactly with another account of the same period from outside the Bible doesn't necessarily mean the Bible is wrong.

4. The New Testament accounts were composed within a generation of the events they record

It is often claimed that the Gospels were written hundreds of years after Jesus' death by fanciful Christians who had never met Jesus, and who embellished the original (much less exciting) stories about him. In other words, an argument that is increasingly advanced these days is that original Christianity was really just about an enigmatic teacher who challenged mainstream Judaism and the imperial Roman ideals of his day; he was a just an ordinary human being who was martyred for his radical teachings. He never rose from the dead and is still buried in Jerusalem somewhere. Then, so the argument goes, over the 1st and 2nd centuries, the accounts about him were slowly embellished by Christians with stories of a miraculous birth and of how he healed the sick, calmed storms, raised the dead and dodged bullets (well, not quite that last one).

These kinds of theories have gained traction in the mainstream media and the entertainment industry because everyone seems to love a good conspiracy theory these days. An obvious example is Dan Brown's best-selling novel (and film) *The Da Vinci Code*.

Yet the vast majority of historians (many of them non-Christian, with no hidden religious agenda), hold firmly to the view that the New Testament documents were all written within the 1st century.

There is a whole field of study filled with academics who are especially devoted to dating the documents of the Bible, and all ancient manuscripts for that matter. This is called "source criticism". In various university laboratories and within the bowels of many museums around the world, groups of nerds (herds of nerds?) work to determine when and where a manuscript was written and what its origin might have been. They study distinctive patterns of handwriting, the language used, the ingredients of the ink, the writing material used (for example, papyrus, pottery, vellum), the style of composition (for example, the column sizes), the content of the document and much more.

Those who are actually in the business of biblical source criticism estimate that the original manuscripts (the first editions) of the New Testament were written within half a century of Jesus being crucified. In fact, a notable portion of those scholars believe that the entire New Testament was written prior to AD 70: that is, within a mere 30-40 years of Jesus' life. That squares with the long-held tradition that Matthew, Mark, Luke and John were all contemporaries of Jesus, with two of them being eyewitnesses themselves. (Matthew and John were both disciples of Jesus.) Those who say that the Gospels were written a hundred years or more after Jesus died are stating something that is quite frankly contrary to the evidence.

5. The Bible hasn't changed over the centuries

Ok, so the *original* documents may have been written soon after Jesus' life—but what about the theory that the

Bible has morphed and changed over the centuries? This argument is usually presented in two different ways.

First of all, it's suggested that influential leaders, particularly in the medieval Roman Catholic church, corrupted and changed the Bible to suit their theology and to control the masses. It's claimed that there were actually only a few copies of the Bible in the world, and they were kept in a secret vault somewhere (perhaps the Vatican), and that crooked churchmen changed the texts for their own devious reasons.

Second, others have claimed that our Bible has derived, slightly more innocently, from a process of transmission like "Chinese whispers" (or the "telephone game", as my American friends know it). This is the idea that scribes simply made mistakes as they copied older manuscripts into new ones, resulting in countless errors compounded through time, so that what we now have in our hands is something far different from the originals.

Let's look at these two commonly held arguments one at a time. In response to the first argument, it's simply not true that the church intentionally changed and edited the actual Bible itself. There is, however, evidence (lots of it, I'm afraid) to show that certain church leaders, of the medieval period in particular, changed their interpretation of the *meaning* of the Bible. Sadly, some churchmen corrupted the Bible's teachings to suit their own purposes in gaining wealth, control and power—in complete contradiction to the very words of Jesus, I might add! But it's incorrect to say that they changed the *actual words* of the Bible itself. There's no real evidence for that, simply because we have so many copies of the biblical manuscripts, dating from the late Middle Ages all the way back to the 2nd and 3rd centuries. Many of these are on public display in various libraries and museums around the world. We can easily compare medieval manuscripts with the 2nd- and 3rd-century manuscripts and see that virtually nothing in the later ones has been changed.

In response to the second argument, the theory that scribes made mistakes, edited the text and omitted whole sections is, well, partly right. But this was not nearly as bad or dramatic as some have said. It is true to say that many copies of the Bible differ slightly from each other. There are *slight* differences in just about all the biblical manuscripts we have. There are minor differences in things like word order or spelling, or sometimes, in rarer cases, one sentence at the end of a paragraph is missing in one or several manuscripts. But the same is true for any collection of manuscripts that we have from the ancient world.

So, for example, on some occasions one manuscript might say "Jesus Christ" while another says "Christ Jesus" or just "Christ." These kinds of "textual variants" can often be traced to scribal errors, but there's virtually no evidence of *theological* changes.

It's worth knowing that ancient and medieval scribes took their work enormously seriously, especially Jewish and Christian scribes copying religious texts. They were ultra-careful in their copying procedures and, in most cases, had their copies double- and triple-checked by a head scribe. Jewish scribal practices included counting the number of words or even counting the number of letters of each document to confirm that the new edition was dead accurate. Yet, despite their meticulous care, scribes, being human, still made the occasional mistake or unintentionally reworded a sentence.

The best English versions of the Bible we have today are all direct translations from the earliest (oldest) manuscripts available worldwide. From Dublin to Jerusalem, Chicago to Sydney, many of the oldest manuscripts of the Bible are on public display in museums and libraries, and a good number of them are dated closely to the originals. (Incidentally, out of the 140 or so earliest manuscripts of the New Testament written on papyri, only two reside in the Vatican Library!)

While it's true that we don't have the original books (first copies, or autographs as they are technically known) of the Bible, that is the case for just about any document from the ancient world. We don't have the original *Iliad* by Homer or Julius Caesar's *Gallic Wars* or Plutarch's *Lives of the Roman Emperors*. No museum or library in the world has the original writings of Socrates, Plato or Aristotle. In fact, we don't even have the originals of any of William Shakespeare's 37 plays. Not one.

What we can confidently say is that we have many copies of the New Testament books that date relatively closely to the originals, and that they haven't been doctored or edited dramatically over the centuries.

So maybe it's worth reassessing your views on the credibility of the Bible. It's far too dismissive to label all Christians as "idiotic", "ignorant" or "unscientific". Many Christians are highly intelligent and hold their faith with great intellectual integrity. There are good, rational reasons to believe in the existence of God and the credibility of the Bible. So it would be more than worth your time to pick it up and try reading it for yourself.

3. Because Christianity is about life to the full

*"To live is the rarest thing in the world.
Most people exist, that is all."*

Oscar Wilde, *The Soul of Man Under Socialism*

I'm sure most of us, at one stage or another, have unknowingly misheard the lyrics of a famous song, and as a result we've been singing the wrong words for years. Apparently, many people still mistakenly sing along to the Eurythmics song "Sweet Dreams" swapping the line "Sweet dreams are made of these" for "Sweet dreams are made of cheese" (which is actually better I reckon). My own personal howler came about in my school days, singing along to the Buggles' song "Video Killed the Radio Star". For years I heard "we can't rewind, we've gone too far", as "with country wine we've gone too far"! I had no idea what "country wine" was, but I presumed the Buggles did, and so I just sang along.

I'm totally convinced that many people reject Christianity because they have been singing the wrong lyrics to the "song of Christianity". They've misheard that Christianity is all about following a set of rules, living a restrictive moral life, going to a boring church on Sunday, abstaining from all fun and praying to a distant God, and then finally heading off to a dreary, cloudy existence called "heaven", to play harps with angels for all eternity.

Basically, people have it in their heads that Christianity is not about life but the end of it.

Now, lyrics can be misheard for a number of reasons: the singer muffles the words, the song is mixed in a way that makes the instruments drown out the vocals, and so on. So why have so many people misheard the lyrics of Christianity?

Well, sometimes it's due to the "performance" of the church. Sadly, in far too many cases, it's Christians themselves who have performed the song of Christianity badly and so have distorted the true lyric of what Jesus actually said and did.

In other cases people claiming to be Christians have actually *deliberately* changed, twisted, or bent the lyrics to suit their own purposes. I'm sure many of us can think of notable tele-evangelists, or those who championed the Crusades in the Middle Ages, or cults or groups like the Ku Klux Klan, all of whom have distorted and changed the true meaning of the Bible to suit their own agendas.

Others have misheard the lyrics of the Christian "song" due to well-meaning but misinformed artists, film-makers and creatives. The first time I ever "saw" Jesus was on TV around Easter in the mid-70s when I was child. I can't remember which film it was, but the Jesus in the movie was just plain weird. He never laughed—in fact, I don't think he even smiled. I continued to watch films like this every Easter up until my mid-teens. All of them seemed to portray Jesus as someone who was never happy and only talked about things I didn't really understand or care about. He certainly wasn't the kind of guy I wanted to hang out with on a day-to-day basis. I was into surfing, sailing, soccer, cricket, riding bikes, hanging out with my mates and chasing girls. What did Jesus have to do with any of that?

Religious art didn't help me either. Most of the art I had seen in books and art galleries represented Jesus as a strangely ethereal, porcelain-skinned, sombre and boring individual. In a majority of the paintings, Jesus was either lying in a manger or dying on a cross, which seemed kind of sad but totally irrelevant to me. I certainly didn't think of life, fun or happiness when it came to the man from Nazareth.

There is another major reason why people mishear lyrics. Sometimes it's not the fault of the band or the singer's accent or the producer's mix; sometimes it's actually the fault of the listener. In some cases, the song is being performed beautifully and clearly but the listener's hearing isn't so good or their sound-system or radio is distorting the track.

In a similar way, many of us misunderstand the lyrics of Christianity because our own hearing is selective— we only half-listen to the words. To be fair, many of us are distracted. We're glued to our favourite sport, or the "white noise" of daily life is drowning out everything else. As a result, many of us only hear a small part of the Christian song at Christmas, Easter, weddings or funerals, but even then, it's only on in the background, so to speak. We're not fully engaged with it; we only hear a small part of the song and dismiss the whole thing on those grounds.

That was certainly the case for me growing up in a non-churchgoing family in Sydney, Australia. I only heard the song of Christianity vaguely once or twice a year as it played faintly in the background of my life. And, if I'm honest, I wasn't trying that hard to listen to it either. I felt I pretty much knew what it was all about and that it wasn't for me. Turns out, like many people, I had completely misheard the lyrics.

THE LYRICS OF CHRISTIANITY

One of the main lyrics of Christianity, which I discovered to my surprise later in life, is that it's all about living life to the fullest.

Yes, you heard that right. Jesus "sang" that on many occasions in multiple ways. He proclaimed that he had come to give us life—real spine-tingling, soul-satisfying life: "life … to the full" (John 10 v 1). He claimed that he

48

had come into this world to bring us happiness, fulfilment joy, meaning, community, purpose, love, hope and more for all eternity. But a lot of people these days don't hear that; in fact, they have misheard the lyric and think Jesus was on about the very opposite.

So in this chapter, I want to lay out three lyrics of Christianity that you may have been mishearing and that I'd love you to consider afresh. These are three words that probably sound to you radically different from what they really mean. That was certainly the case for me. Yet if we stop to listen, we'll discover that Christianity has so much more to offer than we might expect.

"GOD"

The first word is "God". What do you think of when you hear that word?

For many of us, God, if he's there, is not really someone we relate to or would want to hang out with. When I was a kid, I always pictured a crusty old dude with a white beard who sat on a cloud somewhere and looked like Gandalf, but without the charming pipe and warm smile. In my mind he was an eternal grumpy schoolmaster, hovering over us with lightning bolts in one hand and a rule book in the other, ready to send down fire and brimstone on whoever stood out of line.

Many of my non-Christian friends still think along these lines today. Most of them would say, "Why should I be interested in God? He's totally irrelevant to my life and my pursuit of happiness." Most of my friends love going to the pub, watching engaging TV and playing sport. They enjoy fine wine, holidays in Europe and going to gigs to see their favourite bands. They love sitting on beaches, watching sunsets or having a meal at their favourite restaurant. They're serious about coffee, concerned about the environment and passionate about their careers. For them, all this has virtually nothing to do with God and Christianity. They think God is only interested in stained-glass windows, prayer and you being on your best behaviour. In their minds, God has no interest in films, beaches, cooking, modern music or a good cabernet sauvignon—he's just into spiritual things and being boring, and the only things on his playlists are old hymns and organ music.

However, they've drastically misheard the lyric of "God" in the Christian song. The Bible actually presents a God who is far more relevant, exciting and amazing than what we've been led to believe. He's actually into the very things we love and enjoy way more than what we may realise.

One of the best known yet paradoxically most forgotten verses of the Bible when it comes to God is the first one:

In the beginning God created the heavens and the earth.
(Genesis 1 v 1)

Think about that for a moment. Christianity states from its opening line that God made the world—the planet that we so love and enjoy. That verse isn't just an introduction to the Bible; it's an introduction to God. It tells us that he's into stuff—that he is behind the very things we get a kick out of.

God created tropical beaches, coral reefs, alpine meadows and snowfields where we can ski. He made sunsets and sunrises, dolphins, pandas and elephants. He gave us mangos, meat, seafood and coffee beans. He created grapes from which we can make wine and apples so we can bake apple pies. He made cacaos so we could make chocolate and cows from which we make cheese. He crafted rivers for us to go white-water rafting in and lakes for us to sail on. From stars to butterflies, from Everest to the Great Barrier Reef, from the Grand Canyon to the French Alps, God made and gave us all of this!

Moreover, he made us. He created us with the ability to laugh, make friends and fall in love. He designed us with the skills and imagination to create works of art, to write plays, songs and poems, to design cities and to invent technologies.

It seems that many of us, including me, are or have been singing the wrong lyrics about God.

Let me run this by you. What do you think of when you hear the words "the Garden of Eden"? Let's set aside for a moment whether you think the Garden of Eden literally existed or not; what do you have in mind when you think of Eden? Take your time.

Most of us picture a nice place full of colourful flowers, where a naked couple named Adam and Eve frolicked about. You may think of a quaint, flowery garden with a small brook and a few passive animals lying about somewhere: a nice place, but not the sort of place I'd like to hang out in for more than a day or so. After a while, it would get a bit boring.

But if that's what we think, we've misheard the true lyrics. To the Old Testament's first readers living in ancient Israel, a garden wasn't just the place where you read the Sunday paper or lay about catching a few zzzs. The Garden of Eden, as described in the Bible, was a symbol of life and longevity. Eden represented a place of joy, happiness, harmony, wellbeing, food, safety, security, abundant supplies, enjoyable work, rest and play. In short, it was supposed to represent God's generous gift to humanity. It was the perfect home, the perfect work environment and the perfect holiday place all in one location!

Here is the original "lyric" in the second chapter of Genesis:

Now the LORD God had planted a garden in the east, in Eden; and there he put the man he had formed. The LORD God made all kinds of trees grow out of the ground—trees that were pleasing to the eye and good for food. In the middle of the garden were the tree of life and the tree of the knowledge of good and evil. A river watering the garden flowed from Eden; from there it was separated into four headwaters. The name of the first is the Pishon; it winds through the entire land of Havilah, where there is gold. (The gold of that land is good; aromatic resin and onyx are also there.) The name of the second river is the Gihon; it winds through the entire land of Cush. The name of the third river is the Tigris; it runs along the east side of Ashur. And the fourth river is the Euphrates. (Genesis 2 v 8-14)

This brief description is loaded with great details, if we take time to listen. In the ancient world, trees were symbols of life. "All kinds of trees" meant life in abundance. In practical terms, it meant plenty of shade, food and wood for fire and building things.

But notice that the trees in the garden weren't just designed to be useful; they were also "pleasing to the eye", which means that God is also into making things look beautiful. That's good news for artists, architects and designers, or anyone with a creative side. God isn't just about being practical—he cares about how things look aesthetically.

Likewise, multiple rivers in Eden meant the land was fertile and would provide easy irrigation to grow even more trees and crops. Plenty of water meant it was easy to raise livestock and other animals, and that it was a safe place to bring up your family. This aspect was particularly notable for those first readers living in the Middle East, where much of the land was so dry and arid.

The point is that to the ancient reader the Garden of Eden represented the ideal place to live, work and play in. The name of the central tree of Eden sums it up: the tree of life.

This is why, when Genesis began to be translated from Hebrew into ancient Greek (around the middle of the 3rd century BC), Jewish scribes of the day felt that the Greek term for "garden" (*kepos*) didn't quite do the Hebrew text justice. So they borrowed a Persian word instead: "paradeisos", from which we get the word "paradise". Eden was indeed meant to represent the ultimate happy place for everyone. And all this was provided by a generous and wonderfully exciting God.

As a test case, I recently asked one the waitresses at my local café, "What do you think of when you think of the Garden of Eden?" She listed a couple of things but then said, "I think Eden would be a weird and creepy place". Sadly, this is the *very opposite* of what the story of Eden is all about. She had totally misheard the original lyrics of Genesis.

Eden teaches us that God isn't a tyrant who is uninterested in our planet and the things we love and enjoy. It's not that he's solely into spiritual things and only wants us to be on our best behaviour all the time. He created this world and all the beautiful things we love and enjoy to give us a full, blessed life. He gave us the ability to laugh and cry and love. He made us get goosebumps when we hear a great symphony or see an amazing sunset. He gave us taste buds to enjoy tasty food and good coffee. He's not a killjoy or a boring, draconian old man. He gives us great things to enjoy and cares for us.

"JESUS"

Another word (lyric) that I'd love you to reconsider is the name "Jesus". What comes to mind when you hear that name?

In addition to Renaissance art and Easter movies, I can remember that one of the earliest impressions I got of Jesus came from a children's picture Bible. This Bible was actually a lovely gift, given to me by a family close to my own. But for years, whenever I heard the name "Jesus", I'd think of a number of pictures from this children's Bible, and one in particular. It was a pastel watercolour picture of Jesus sitting on a rock in the middle of a flowery meadow, surrounded by daisies, squirrels, robins and a couple of lambs. At his feet sat a ring of small, immaculately dressed children all looking intently at Jesus. Basically, Jesus looked like a male version of Maria von Trapp out of *The Sound of Music*. Jesus' mouth was open and he was telling those kids something. In my mind, he was telling those kids a parable about a good Samaritan, three bears and a wicked Pharisee, and the moral of the story was that they should eat all their vegetables and not run with scissors.

I don't know what image comes to your mind when you think of Jesus. For many people, he's a bit like what I've just described: a Disney cartoon character or a strange tree-hugging hippy from the 1960s or some kind of moral crusader. To be fair, some of my non-churchgoing friends give Jesus a bit more credit than that. For them he is a philosopher/guru: a kind of blend between Gandhi and the Dalai Lama. They would happily tell you that he had interesting things to say (even though they don't know what he actually said) and that he might be worth having over to a dinner party one evening. But for most of them, as far as real life in the 21st century goes, Jesus is totally irrelevant.

But I would love to suggest again that many of us have misheard the lyric of "Jesus" and what he was really all about.

Take, for example, the first miracle Jesus performed, when he turned water into wine. (You can read about it in the Gospel of John, chapter 2.) For starters, it's worth pointing out that Jesus turned water into wine, not the other way round. He didn't take something good that we enjoy and turn it into something plain and boring. He took water out of six huge ceremonial washing jars and turned it into wine for enjoyment. And not just any wine—really good wine.

Furthermore, he did it at a wedding party, in order to keep the party going. Jesus wasn't the party pooper I long thought he was. Turns out he was the party starter!

The book's author, John, points out that this was Jesus' *first* miracle, which prompts a question: why did Jesus launch his ministry with a miracle at a party? Why choose to do it that way?

Well, because it was a brilliant, vivid picture of what his ministry and the kingdom of God were all about. His kingdom, the place where he hangs out, is full of life, fun, happiness and joy. He was teaching everyone there that he had come to invite people to a party. Later he would go on to say, on several occasions, that the kingdom of God is like a royal wedding feast and that we're all invited!

To show us what the "party" was going to be like, he went on to heal people from all sorts of illnesses and diseases, giving them their dignity again as he restored them to health. He sat and dined with prostitutes, outcasts and the irreligious, giving them hope and offering forgiveness. He plugged people back into their communities and back into God. He gave people meaning and purpose as he taught about life—life to the fullest. Jesus' ministry, in many ways, was one giant preview of the biggest party ever in the next world. The turning of water into wine at a wedding banquet was only the start.

In chapter 15 of the Gospel of Luke, Jesus told three stories back to back: of a shepherd who had lost a sheep, a woman who had lost a coin and a father who had lost a rebellious son. All three scenarios are stories of reunification: the shepherd finds his lost sheep, the woman finds her lost coin, and the prodigal son eventually comes home to his father. Significantly, in all three stories, there is a party at the end. The shepherd, the woman and the father each throw a big party when what was lost is found. *That's what God's kingdom is like*, said Jesus. It's about reconciliation with God and being invited in to enjoy his "party" for ever.

"HEAVEN"

The final lyric I'd love you to hear afresh is the word "heaven". Most of my non-churchgoing friends would say they picture heaven as people walking around in long, white nightgowns, floating on fluffy clouds and listening to dated choral music, like you might get in a department store elevator. They picture a place of ethereal tranquillity that looks relaxing but, in the end, is pretty boring. That's certainly how I used to picture it. Even as a young Christian, when I thought of heaven, I wasn't that excited about it. While it was clearly better than "the other place", it wasn't something I looked forward to. But yet again, I'd been singing the wrong lyric.

Perhaps the closest thing we have to a "brochure" on heaven is found in the last few chapters of the Bible in the book of Revelation. In symbolic picture language, the author (again, the apostle John) describes a vision in which he was taken on a tour of the afterlife by some angelic guide and given a glimpse of what life would look like for God's people for eternity. Here's part of the original lyric:

Then I saw "a new heaven and a new earth," for the first heaven and the first earth had passed away, and there was no longer any sea. I saw the Holy City, the new Jerusalem, coming down out of heaven from God, prepared as a bride beautifully dressed for her husband. And I heard a loud voice from the throne saying, "Look! God's dwelling-place is now among the people, and he will dwell with them. They will be his people, and God himself will be with them and be their God. 'He will wipe every tear from their eyes. There will be no more death' or mourning or crying or pain, for the old order of things has passed away." ...

Then the angel showed me the river of the water of life, as clear as crystal, flowing from the throne of God and of the Lamb down the middle of the great street of the city. On each side of the river stood the tree of life, bearing twelve crops of fruit, yielding its fruit every month. And the leaves of the tree are for the healing of the nations.

(Revelation 21 v 1-4; 22 v 1-2)

Admittedly, the significance of the details is hard to understand in parts, even for the most learned of theologians. Sometimes this description reads a bit more like something that Tolkien or C.S. Lewis would have written, but it's easy to get the gist of it.

The first thing to notice here is that there's no mention of choral music, fluffy clouds, unicorns, nightgowns, or harps and halos. Most importantly, there's absolutely no indication whatsoever of this place being dull or boring.

The other thing not to miss is that the next life, or "heaven" as we might call it, is physical. The Bible—both here and elsewhere—speaks of eternal life for God's people on a "new earth". The next world will be exactly that—a world! Presumably, then, it will be a place where we will play, walk, run, swim, eat, drink and live life to the fullest—a physical place where there are trees, rivers, skies (heavens) and so on. That said, you might have noticed that John says that "there was no longer any sea". For many years, I thought this sounded pretty disappointing, until I discovered that the "sea" represented chaos and instability to the ancient reader. It's therefore not saying that in the next life there'll be no bodies of water, but that there will no longer be any turmoil, chaos and disorder. Instead, John sees a city, which represents a home, community, safety and security.

Most significantly, God is in uninhibited communion with humanity. John gets a glimpse of how God and people are meant to be, with no tears, or pain or suffering anymore. It is, in many ways, a new Eden. Just think about that for a moment. All those things that make us sad, angry or anxious—gone. No more crime, poverty, greed or family break-ups. Disease and death will become things of the past.

This whole vision is meant to tell us that life with God is going to be the best time ever. It will be the "life to the full" that Jesus talked about, for all eternity—the very opposite of what many of us have been hearing.

WORTH LISTENING

So, maybe for years you've misheard the original lyric of Christianity. In your mind, the song of Christianity was always about rules, religiosity and a life of perpetual boredom. I hope by now you've heard at least some of the lyrics afresh. But please, keep listening—there's so much more to hear. Christianity is not about the suppression of life but about embracing it. It's about the very things we all long for: hope, joy, love, meaning, safety, fulfilment, and happiness because, when we stop to consider the original lyrics, we find that Jesus' life, teaching and ministry overflowed with those very things.

4. Because Christianity gives a compelling answer to the question "What's wrong with the world?"

"People often claim to hunger for truth, but seldom like the taste when it's served up."

George R.R. Martin, *A Clash of Kings*

I think most of us can agree that the world is a pretty messed-up place. I'm sure I don't need to labour the point. No matter where you live in the world, you'd be hard pressed to watch half an hour of one of your main news channels without seeing at least something on war, crime, terrorism, racism, poverty, slavery or some human-induced environmental disaster.

I currently live in London, one of the most beautiful and prosperous cities on the planet, and yet I'm surrounded by greed, racism, suffering, injustice, sexism, animal cruelty, robberies and an alarming increase in street crime. This year is proving to be one of the worst on record for knife crime in London. Even as I write this, I'm hearing reports on the news of yet another young person who was fatally stabbed overnight. The victim was chased, beaten and finally knifed to death. He was just 17 years old.

Added to our treatment of each other, there's our collective treatment of the planet. Collectively, we've carelessly caused the extinction of hundreds of animals, destroyed precious forests and filled the oceans with plastic. The United Nations Environment Programme estimates that we're dumping at least 8 million tons of plastic into our oceans every year! Apparently, more than half of all sea turtles have consumed plastic debris in some form or another, and we're destroying our coral reefs on a daily basis. Sadly, according to WWF (World Wide Fund for Nature), there are presently around 20 animals on the critically endangered list. One of the most beautiful among them is the Amur leopard, a rare species of big cat desperately trying to cling on to existence. Apparently, there are fewer than 100 left in the world.

I think we all agree that our world is broken in multiple ways. But what we can't agree on is why. What's the root cause of all this brokenness, and how do we fix it?

THE DOCTOR'S ASSESSMENT

I'm no doctor, but I'm pretty sure the best way to heal someone is to first correctly diagnose the problem. There's no point in giving someone medicine for a stomach ulcer when they're suffering from a broken foot. Or extracting a tooth when they've got a sore arm. In order to work out the right remedy for something, you first have to work out the right malady.

So what's the problem with humanity? What's wrong with the world? What's causing all this crime, suffering, destruction and chaos? Well, there's a smorgasbord of answers. People tend to lay the blame for our problems at the foot of at least one or a combination of the following:

- the inequality of social classes

- the government

- poverty

- capitalism

- a lack of education

- not enough gun control

- religious extremism

- the internet

- a lack of love

- a breakdown of the family unit

- gender or racial inequality

You may think of other reasons, or maybe you don't really know.

I believe that Christianity offers the most sobering and accurate diagnosis of all. Essentially, the blame for what's wrong with the world doesn't lie with any of the things listed above. According to the core teachings of Jesus, these are the *symptoms* of the problem, not the root cause—just as a headache or stomach pains aren't usually the root of the problem but the symptoms of something deeper (such as dehydration or food poisoning or a virus).

The Christian diagnosis of the problem of the world is that all human beings, in some form or another, have a "virus" which distorts us and eventually kills us. The great problem of the world isn't just what we do; it's *who we are*. According to Jesus and the Bible, we're all broken in some way, infected with the virus of "sin". It's in the DNA of our souls. Within all of us, there's at least some form of arrogance, over-confidence, self-centredness and greed. And, if we're honest, we have the track record to prove it. History is our CV, and it's not a good read.

Sure, we often do good things; I'm not saying we don't. Most of us show kindness, compassion, charity and love on a daily basis. We can be caring towards others much of the time (when we're on form). But we can also exhibit cold-heartedness, selfishness, impatience, vanity, lust, greed, hatred and much more, sometimes even in the same moment.

Apparently, around 58% of us have lied on our resumés to get a job over someone else.[6] Perhaps as many as half of us have been unfaithful to a partner.[7] As many as two-thirds of us have stolen something from work, and most of us, at one point or another, have broken the law. According to Douglas Husak, an American law scholar of Rutgers University in New Jersey, as many as 70% of us have committed a crime that could have led to imprisonment.

"Sure," you might be thinking, "but that's not me". The problem is that most of us measure our "goodness" by our own standards, not God's. We can think, "I'm a nice guy" or "I'm a considerate person" without really seeing some harsh truths about our own lives. Let me offer just one of my own shortcomings as Exhibit A.

I often pride myself on my ability to stand patiently in a queue. Jumping a queue is one of the greatest crimes you can commit in Britain. I find it not only inconsiderate but enormously offensive, particularly when I've been patiently waiting in line for a long time. Yet, on quite a few occasions, sometimes at an airport or at a gig, I have bent this golden rule for my own needs. I have stifled my own conscience and knowingly queue-jumped at the expense of others. And yes, that's a rather trivial example, but that's because it's the only example I'm willing to give you—there are plenty more serious ones.

In Jesus' day, the religious elite prided themselves on their own goodness: not just for standing in line correctly, but in just about everything they did. They were proud of keeping the laws of the Old Testament and of their own supposed godliness. As result, they felt pretty good about themselves. The trouble was that they were measuring themselves by their *own standards*, not God's. They thought they were being charitable, but actually they were only charitable to people they found culturally acceptable. They thought they were concerned for God, but actually they were much more concerned for their own reputations. They thought they were morally pure, but their morality was only skin deep. It wasn't until Jesus confronted them that their true internal morality (or lack of it) was dramatically exposed.

This is one of the lessons in Jesus' famous "Sermon on the Mount" and is the reason why, to this day, it's still so enduringly powerful. During the sermon, Jesus taught that all of us are morally impaired. Every single one of us. No one is good completely. No one can keep all the Ten Commandments: not even the ones like *do not murder* and *do not commit adultery* (Exodus 20 v 1-17). He basically said that you're an adulterer at heart when you lust after someone, even though you have never slept with them. You're a murder when you hate someone, even if you haven't killed them. While we may not commit the crime physically, the intent is lying there deep within our hearts.

The problem is that we don't always see (or want to see) the problem.

My wife and I used to have a bathroom in which the ceiling light had three light bulbs. From time to time one of the bulbs would blow, and my wife would ask me to replace it. But often I would try to put it off—not out of laziness (well, maybe in part) but because with just the two bulbs, when I looked in the mirror, I looked cleaner and, quite frankly, a bit younger. After some time, another light bulb would blow, leaving just one, after which I looked literally half my age. The blemishes and wrinkles had miraculously disappeared!

People often feel that they're a good person because they're standing in the room of their own limited conscience, darkened by their culture and their own flexible standards. We feel pretty good about ourselves because of the distorted principles we've created to suit our own desires. But when we see what Christ was like, and when we listen to what he had to say about ethics, goodness, kindness, humility, love and self-sacrifice, we realise that we've been looking into a darkened mirror our whole life. When you're confronted with the life and teachings of Jesus, it's like suddenly having a mirror held up to your face with all the light bulbs in the room turned on. Only then do you realise that you're not so good, clean, loving, kind, charitable and considerate after all.

THE HEART OF THE PROBLEM

It's often been said that "the heart of the human problem is the problem of the human heart."[8] That diagnosis actually originates from the teachings of Jesus. Speaking to his disciples he said:

For out of the heart come evil thoughts—murder, adultery, sexual immorality, theft, false testimony, slander.
(Matthew 15 v 19)

The film director and producer Bette Gordon was once interviewed about her film *The Drowning*, adapted from the novel *Border Crossing* by Pat Barker. The novel tells the story of Tom Seymour, a forensic psychologist haunted by a past case in which his expert testimony sealed the fate of a young boy who was consequently sent to prison. In the interview Gordon was asked what drew her to the story and made her want to turn it into a film. She gave this honest reply:

"After a tragic incident, in which a close friend was murdered by her 19-year-old son, I was given [the novel] 'Border Crossing'. When I read it, I knew I wanted to make it into a film. The book explores the question of evil—if it can ever really be explained, let alone treated ...

"As a culture, we are horrified and at the same time fascinated by the dark side of human nature. We consume media that focuses on evil characters. We read books about it, we want to lock it behind bars, exorcise it, and quarantine it, but we don't look away. Maybe that's because there is an implicit awareness that there is a darkness in all of us."[9]

Or, as the 19th-century author Mark Twain once put it:

"Everyone is a moon, and has a dark side which he never shows to anybody."[10]

Now, some of my atheist friends would say to me at this point, "Oh, there you go again—another religious argument that makes us all feel guilty and terrible". In fact, some of them have told me that they don't go to church because of this very reason—they'll leave feeling guilty and depressed. "Why would I go to church just to hear how rotten I am?" they say.

I get that—but I wish they'd stick around and hear the rest of the story. Otherwise it's like walking out of the doctor's surgery before they get to the good news about the great cure that's available.

AGREEING WITH THE ASSESSMENT

But before we get to Christianity's cure, it's worth pointing out that there's something good in being given an accurate diagnosis of our problem. Again, as when we go to the doctor, don't we all want an accurate assessment of our condition? When it comes to our health, we want the truth, even if it's not the kind of news we like to hear.

Actually, it can be quite liberating when we admit our faults and shortcomings. There's something freeing about looking at your life with open honesty. One of my favourite comments on this topic comes from the civil rights campaigner Martin Luther King Jr. There's something beautifully honest and humble in these words:

"In every one of us, there's a war going on. It's a civil war. I don't care who you are, I don't care where you live, there is a civil war going on in your life. And every time you set out to be good, there's something pulling on you, telling you to be evil. It's going on in your life. Every time you set out to love, something keeps pulling on you, trying to get you to

hate. Every time you set out to be kind and say nice things about people, something is pulling on you to be jealous and envious and to spread evil gossip about them … There's a tension at the heart of human nature. And whenever we set out to dream our dreams and to build our temples, we must be honest enough to recognise it."[11]

The Bible gives this very sobering yet powerful answer to the question: "What's wrong with the world?"

It's you and me.

We're all broken and corrupt, and while that's hard to hear (especially at first), it's also surprisingly liberating to be given an accurate diagnosis and to go on to humbly accept it.

HOW AND WHEN DID WE BECOME BROKEN?

However, you may well ask, "If this is the condition of all humanity, how did we get here?" The answer is given to us in the early chapters of Genesis, told semi-pictorially in the story of the creation of the world and the Garden of Eden. In those first chapters of the Bible we read of God gifting humankind (represented in Adam and Eve) with the ability to choose between right and wrong, between following God or following their own instincts and desires. They chose autonomy—and now we all have too. It's as if we've all taken part in a referendum and each one of us has voted to "leave" God. We've all walked away from him, and the rest of history has been the result of humans living by our own standards without God in the way.

Curiously, *eating* is significant in the Genesis story. Adam and Eve ate the fruit from the tree they were forbidden to eat. They didn't just look at it or touch it—they ate it. That strikingly symbolises a total *ingestion of rebellion* that has gone deep into our inner being. The point of the story is that through our own pride and arrogance, we've completely poisoned ourselves, and we're now suffering the symptoms.

In his marvellous little book *Mere Christianity*, C.S. Lewis has a chapter called "The Great Sin". The book is worth getting for this chapter alone. In it he says that the "great sin"—the origin of all sin—is pride. We think we know better than our Creator. We've effectively fired him from his job, taken on the role of chief decision-maker for our lives and poisoned ourselves in the process.

The result of sin in our lives has been catastrophic. According to the story contained in Genesis 3, four things break as a result of our pride:

1. Our relationship with God is broken

The relationship of harmony between God and humankind (represented in Adam and Eve) was destroyed. Adam and Eve were cast out of the paradise of Eden, and most importantly, cast away from God's presence. In effect, God was saying, "You cannot enjoy the gift of paradise if you refuse the Giver of paradise." We all distrust God and ignore his guidelines for life; our relationship with him is broken.

2. Our relationships with others are broken

The second consequence of sinful pride in the story of Eden is discord between human beings. Adam blamed Eve, and their relationship was marred with shame. The same pattern was passed on to their children; in the very next chapter, Cain kills his brother Abel. We've seen disharmony and conflict within our families, in our communities and between countries ever since.

3. Our bodies are broken

The third result of walking away from God is that our bodies are decaying and eventually will cease to function. Basically, we die. Before Adam and Eve rebelled against their Creator, God warned them that if they walked away from him, they and their offspring would die and be separated from God for ever (being cast out of Eden represented being cut off from life). This is much like a roving astronaut umbilically attached to a space station; come undone and you may survive for a while in your spacesuit, but your existence is unsustainable. Eventually you'll run out of heat and oxygen, and you'll die. Consequently, as rebels against our Creator, we all suffer from sickness, pain and disease, and eventually we go to the grave. But if that wasn't bad enough, the Bible also talks about death in spiritual terms. Basically, *rebellion against God results in an experience of eternal death beyond the grave*, with no hope of heaven. As our Creator and Sustainer, he's the life support system we all need to be plugged into, but if you unplug yourself from him you will eventually die eternally.

4. Our world is broken

The fourth consequence of our rebellion against God is often missed by many Christians, but it's there in the story. When Adam and Eve decided to go it alone, God cursed the ground; this was symbolic of a broken world. Nature itself was spoiled and continues to malfunction in various ways. When we see decay, destruction and chaos, it's a striking visual reminder that this is a world gone wrong.

In the pages that follow Genesis 3—through historical events, parables, songs and sermons—the Bible graphically teaches us about sin and its consequences, drawing on numerous terms and images. In *moral* terms, we're sons and daughters of disobedience: corrupt, immoral and essentially evil. In *navigational* terms, we're lost and have wandered from the path like sheep. In *relational* terms, we've flirted with evil and played the harlot, and committed spiritual adultery. In *medical* terms, we're all blind, deaf, leprous, paralysed and even dead. In *hygiene* terms, we're unclean, dirty, polluted and stained in our hearts. In *judicial* terms, we all stand guilty in the divine courts of justice. And in *financial* terms, we've all racked up an insurmountable debt that we can never pay, and thus we're all spiritually bankrupt. It's a pretty arresting analysis!

Now, I'm sorry to kick you when you're down, but the Christian assessment of our condition gets worse. Here's the thing: *we can't heal ourselves*. We may be able to stem the blood flow, so to speak, or improve our collective quality of life through "palliative care"—using laws, rules, punishments and incentives—but we can't totally fix the root of the problem. We all have a serious heart problem that requires surgery that we can't perform on ourselves.

Christianity is virtually unique regarding this aspect of its assessment of the human condition. In just about any religion of the world, there is a belief that somehow, in some way, we can heal, restore and save ourselves. In Buddhism, there is the eight-fold path towards enlightenment and inner peace. In Islam, there are the five pillars to adhere to so that one hopefully reaches paradise. Even atheists have their solutions. For example, some may say, "What we need are better educational programmes, or a better system of government, or the eradication of poverty..." If only we could do *this* or *that*, the thinking goes, then we will have happiness and harmony.

But will we really ever get there? Have we ever come close? Are things actually getting better? The trouble is that increasing wealth and improved educational programmes haven't ultimately helped us—not totally. Let's not forget that many of the leaders of the Nazi Party, the very men who built and ran death camps like Auschwitz and Dachau, were some of the most well-educated and wealthiest men in Europe. Many of them had read the classics, sat in concert halls listening to Mozart, Chopin and the like, and had college degrees and even doctorates; yet they were still capable of the most heinous crimes in history. Likewise, some of the most notorious criminals of the last 100 years were highly educated and sophisticated people. As one saying goes, "Educate a devil and you don't get an angel; you just get a very clever devil". Is a better education or more money or culture *really* the solution to our problems?

The Bible, on the other hand, teaches that we can't ultimately fix ourselves by anything we do, be that education, discipline or even religious laws. While Christianity does indeed teach its followers to love their neighbour and be kind, charitable and compassionate to others, the Bible also teaches that these good deeds won't entirely solve the problem of the human heart and therefore our world. The Old Testament is basically one massive lesson in how commandments and laws may help stem the symptoms of the disease of sin but will *never ultimately fix it*. The heart of the human problem cannot be solved with a plaster cast of rules. What's required is a totally new heart, or, as Jesus taught, to be born again: to become a new person. Changing metaphors, what we need is a total reboot: an installation of a completely new operating system and hard drive in every single one of us.

We'll see more about this in the chapters ahead. The point of this one is that Christianity is worth considering because it gives us the most accurate diagnosis of our problems and the best answer to the question "What's wrong with our world?"

The answer: I am.

5. Because Jesus is arguably the most influential person in history

"I am an historian, I am not a believer, but I must confess as a historian that this penniless preacher from Nazareth is irrevocably the very centre of history. Jesus Christ is easily the most dominant figure in all history."

H.G. Wells (author of *The War of the Worlds*)

Who would you list as the top three most influential people in history?

A few years ago, Wikipedia put together a list of the most influential people in history, based on their Wikipedia entry's PageRank. (Yes, I had to look that up. Apparently, it's a type of algorithm named after Larry Page, the co-founder of Google, that assesses internet pages by the number of other pages that link to them.)

Their results might surprise you.

At number 3 was Aristotle.

At number 2 was Jesus.

And at number 1, the most influential person that ever lived was... Carl Linnaeus (an 18th-century Swedish scientist and botanist). You may well have heard of him, but I must confess that I most definitely had not.

Yet despite Jesus missing out on the top spot in that particular list, it's still reasonable to argue that he is the most talked about, sung about, and written about person in all of world history. From Mozart to U2, he has been the inspiration for more musicians than any other person that's ever lived. He's the subject of more paintings and sculptures, books and essays, Hollywood blockbusters and TV documentaries than any other figure in history.

But he's not just *famous*; Jesus has been deeply influential. Jesus' words have shaped cultures, countries, presidents, kings, queens and emperors. Some of his words and teachings have been the basis for laws and whole judicial systems. He has inspired schools, orphanages, hospitals, universities, civil-rights movements and charities worldwide for two millennia. He is easily the most studied, debated, worshipped, followed, talked about person that has ever lived. And if that's the case, isn't it worth finding out more about what he had to say about life, and what he did with his own?

He's worth thinking about because no one else—no monarch, dictator, scientist, educator, philosopher, Nobel Prize recipient, CEO, sportsperson or religious leader—

has made a greater impact on world history than Jesus Christ. Billions of people have come and gone on this planet—from Julius Caesar to Elon Musk, Joan of Arc to Catherine the Great, Plato to Nelson Mandela—but no one comes close to equalling the influence which the carpenter from Nazareth has had in the world.

Not convinced about how famous Jesus is? Let me put it another way. Let me list a few famous people from the entire span of recorded history and then get you (without Googling) to think of what you know about them. Some of them you'll recognise instantly, some of them may be vaguely familiar to you and, I'm guessing, that there'll be others you've never heard of at all. But they have all been very famous, at least at one point or another. Here's the list:

Ramses II, Homer, Cyrus of Persia, Pythagoras, Alexander the Great, Julius Caesar, Cleopatra VII, Boudicca, Constantine, Genghis Kahn, Marco Polo, Mansa Musa, Johann Guttenberg, Joan of Arc, Christopher Columbus, Leonardo Da Vinci, Martin Luther, Suleiman the Magnificent, William Shakespeare, Elizabeth I, Isaac Newton, Catherine the Great, George Washington, Napoleon, Charles Darwin, Ada Lovelace, Queen Victoria, Harriet Tubman, Thomas Edison, Winston Churchill, Albert Einstein, Chairman Mao, Don Bradman, Mother Teresa, Ella Fitzgerald, Nelson Mandela, Queen Elizabeth II, Valentina Tereshkova, Stephen Hawking, Muhammad Ali, Meryl Streep, Angela Merkel, Bill Gates, Martina Navratilova, Michael Jackson, Barack Obama, Michael Jordan, Adele.

How did you do? There are probably quite a few names there that are familiar to you and about whom you know something. But of how many in that list can you say you know where they were born? Or who their mother was? Or what their most famous sayings were? Or (where applicable) how they died?

Here's my point: even if you don't know much about Jesus, most people can still tell you where he was born (Bethlehem), when he was born (a little over 2,000 years ago), who his mother was (Mary), where he grew up (Nazareth in Galilee), at least one thing he famously said ("Blessed are the peacemakers", "Do not judge", "Turn the other cheek", "Love one another"), and how he died (on a Roman cross). Way above anyone in that list, Jesus is still easily the most famous person in all of history. Surely, if you're a thinking person and have at least some desire to understand the world in which we live, then you'll want to have a working knowledge of such an influential figure, beyond the basic trivia.

So, what should you know about Jesus? Why is he so influential? It seems to me that Jesus is famous and important to so many people for essentially two reasons: What he *said* and what he *did*, as both point to who he is. Let's look at them one at a time.

WHAT HE SAID: WORDS OF CONVICTION

Jesus is worth considering simply for what he said—and not just what he said, but the way in which he said it.

Regardless of what one thinks of the content of what he taught, Jesus was undeniably a master communicator. His teachings and oratory skills have been admired by people of all religions and none—from the Dalai Lama to Bill Clinton and from Gandhi to Jay-Z. Even Richard Dawkins, one of the most prominent so-called "New Atheists", and author of *The God Delusion*, has said that "Jesus was a great moral teacher".[12]

Jesus attracted thousands of people from all over ancient Judea, who came to hear him preach. He could hold an audience for hours on end speaking on a whole range of topics: from life to death, heaven to hell and marriage to divorce. He spoke about taxes, wealth, poverty and injustice, all with equally assured confidence. He could demolish the arguments of his theological opponents with just a simple question, leaving them to scurry away with their tails between their legs. His parables are regarded as masterpieces of rhetoric. He was the master spokesmen, orator, preacher, teacher and debater.

If we take the New Testament accounts of Jesus' life at face value, there was no backwardness or shyness about what he had to say. He was totally self-assured in who he was and what he had to say on any given subject. There is no indication in the Gospels that Jesus was on a learning curve or that he felt he was on a "spiritual journey". There's no suggestion that he struggled for answers or was thrown by the arguments of his enemies.

Put simply, he spoke with great confidence and conviction. Jesus unblushingly said of himself, "I am the gate" (John 10 v 9), "I am the light of the world" (John 8 v 12), and "I am the good shepherd" (John 10 v 11). He never said, "I *think* I'm the good shepherd" or "I'm *reasonably confident* that I am the gate", or "I'm still on a path to figuring it all out". It was always "*I am...*" without a shadow of a doubt.

WORDS OF CONTROVERSY

But Jesus was and is far more famous for what he said than the way he said it. His teachings were and are enormously controversial—mainly because they're exclusive. Jesus claimed that he, and he alone, is "the way and the truth and the life" and that no one can get to heaven except through him (John 14 v 6). He didn't say that he was *a* way but "*the* way"; not *a* light of the world but "*the* light of the world". That effectively wipes out every other religion going and still, to this day, remains offensive. I live in London, one of the most multi-cultural cities in the world, where exclusive claims of that nature are basically off-limits. Yet, that's what Jesus boldly said about himself. These were massively provocative claims. You can't soften those statements. He was either right or he was wrong.

There were other things too that Jesus said that got under peoples' skin back then. In both private discussions with the disciples and public talks before the crowds, Jesus claimed that he was not only sent by God himself but that he would die and rise from the dead, and finally one day return and judge the world. As you can imagine, in

Jesus' day that not only raised theological eyebrows but got him into a lot of hot water. In fact, he not only claimed that he had been sent from heaven by the Father, but he kept pointing to the fact that he was literally God himself ("Anyone who has seen me has seen the Father", John 14 v 9). It was perhaps this claim above all others that led to his eventual arrest, trial and execution.

Jesus also made the similarly outlandish claim that while he would one day judge the world, he was initially here to save it: "I did not come to judge the world, but to save the world" (John 12 v 47). On numerous occasions, and in various ways, Jesus said that he came for a great purpose: "to seek and to save the lost" (Luke 19 v 10). Similarly, he proclaimed that he had come to give life to the full (John 10 v 10) and that he would do this, paradoxically, by dying. He said that he "did not come to be served, but to serve, and to give his life as a ransom for many" (Mark 10 v 45).

Jesus uncompromisingly claimed that he had come to save the world and restore it, through dying and rising again. We'll see more about this in the next chapters, but the point here is that Jesus confidently and rather controversially taught that he was divine and that he came for a purpose—to save the world.

So, here's what I'd like you to (re)consider: Jesus was who he said he was, or he wasn't. Either he was God in human form and came to rescue the world, or he wasn't. Either he was right when he said that he was "the way, the truth and the life", or he was wrong. There's no in-between.

As the author C.S. Lewis put it, Jesus was either a "lunatic", a "liar" or Lord—he was either a delusional mad-man, a great con-artist who deceived people into following him, or God himself, walking in our shoes.[13] If you come to the conclusion that he was telling the truth and he really was God in human form here on earth, then that changes everything.

WHAT HE DID: JESUS' CONDUCT

"Ok," you might be thinking, "but history shows us that there have been plenty of lunatics and liars who have gained a following." After all, it's one thing to confidently claim that you've been sent from heaven and that you're here to save the world, but it's another thing all together to then go on to prove it.

Here's the thing: Jesus did. The claim of the New Testament authors is that Jesus, very conclusively and very publicly, backed up his claims and teachings with his conduct and miracles. His actions gave great credibility to his words.

Jesus' ethic of love and compassion for all, and turning the other cheek when wronged, was beautifully and consistently modelled in his own life. He sat and dined with those who were marginalised and despised and the outcasts of his day. In fact, his enemies labelled him "a friend of ... sinners" (Matthew 11 v 19). He spent long hours listening to and helping people of questionable character, often shunning his own comfort and at great cost to his own reputation. At times he often endured harsh and misinformed criticism without retaliating. He really did practise what he preached.

In fact, no one seemed able to pin any "dirt" on him at all. Even at his trial, none of the mud slung at him managed to stick. He was the friend of sinners but abstained from being one himself. He didn't lie or steal or gossip, or do anything that contradicted what he himself taught.

He told people to help the poor and beware of the love of money, and he modelled that exquisitely. Thus, there is no indication whatsoever that he owned much. He didn't have a big farm or the finest fishing boat or a couple of the latest chariots in his garage. He didn't even seem to own a donkey (since in Matthew 21 v 1-3 he had to borrow one!). Curiously, not one of his enemies, even at his trial, accused him of being a hypocrite. Jesus walked the walk as well as talking the talk.

JESUS' MIRACLES

Perhaps most notable of all of Jesus' actions were his miracles. These not only acted as previews of the eternal kingdom that Jesus had come to bring about, they were also tangible, public "proofs" for what he was saying. When Jesus claimed he was "the light of the world", he proved it by opening the eyes of blind people. When he said that he was "the bread of life", he miraculously fed 5,000 people with a few loaves of bread and a couple of fish (John 6). Perhaps most impressively of all, when he said that he was "the resurrection and the life", he followed it up by raising Lazarus from the dead and then went on to rise from the grave himself. Basically, the miracles were his "I told you so".

Now, I know what you're probably thinking at this stage: are we honestly expected to believe in this day and age that Jesus really *could* do all those science-suspending miracles? For most people these days, the alleged miracles of Jesus in the Gospels ironically make him seem *less* credible, when they were supposed to do the very opposite and prove his credibility.

However, that kind of argument, in and of itself, is a little unfair. If I showed up at your house and was seriously claiming that I was God in human form, the next thing you'd probably say to me is "Prove it!" You'd want me to do something to back it up. If I couldn't pull off anything miraculous, then you'd have every right to say to me, "I don't believe you're God!" That's why the first eyewitnesses tell us that Jesus backed up his words with multiple jaw-dropping, eye-popping, spine-chilling, science-defying miracles. If he *didn't* do them, then we'd have every right to be at least suspicious of his claims. Yet paradoxically, these days, if we say he did do miracles, people *don't* believe.

So let's not miss the argument of the New Testament authors. They claimed that Jesus was divine: not just because he claimed it but because he displayed it. They knew that the best way for someone to affirm divinity was by doing something divine. Or put another way, if Jesus didn't do any miracles whatsoever, why should anyone have confidence that he was telling the truth?

It's worth knowing that the authors of the four Gospels (Matthew, Mark, Luke and John) used several different Greek words for what we call "miracles". One of the most common words was *dynameis* (mighty works), related to our English word "dynamite". Another word was *terata* (wonders, miracles). More often than not, John preferred the word *semeia* (signs) for the miracles (which is related to our word "*sign*ificant"). I like this term in particular because a "sign" is meant point us to something or, in this case, *someone*! These incredible miraculous "signs" are meant to point out to us that Jesus was who he claimed to be.

This is all the more striking given that the first followers of Jesus were almost all Jewish. To an orthodox Jew (and, today, a Muslim), the idea that God would become a man and dine with sinners was not only absurd but also unequivocally blasphemous. In other words, Jesus' Jewish disciples would have faced not one but two obstacles to believing he was God in human form. Not only would they have had rational reasons for doubting that Jesus could be divine, but they would have had huge theological objections as well. In fact, the disciples then would have needed to be convinced of his divinity *more than anyone else in the Roman Empire*. That the first Christians who worshipped a carpenter's son from Nazareth as the Son of God were from a *Jewish* background is no small thing. They wouldn't have come to that conclusion lightly. Yet, the miracles seemed to have been the major turning point for them. By seeing the miracles for themselves, they became utterly convinced that they were looking at someone who truly was divine.

Here are three things I'd like you to (re)consider about Jesus' miracles:

1. There were many miracles

What is very impressive to many is the sheer scope of Jesus' miraculous actions. He didn't just heal one or two people, or heal people from the same illness (like a travelling showman repeating the same trick over and over again). He healed hundreds of people suffering from all sorts of different maladies, so much so that sometimes the Gospel writers just have to summarise his miraculous activity by saying simply that Jesus healed many others. For example, Mark describes an evening when "the whole town gathered at the door, and Jesus healed many who had various diseases" (Mark 1 v 33-34).

John concludes his account by saying:

Jesus performed many other signs in the presence of his disciples, which are not recorded in this book. But these are written that you may believe that Jesus is the Messiah, the Son of God, and that by believing you may have life in his name. (John 20 v 30-31)

There are around 40 miracles recorded for us in some detail in the Gospels. We have the accounts of people being healed from blindness, deafness and other illnesses like leprosy or curvature of the spine; we're also told that Jesus raised at least three people from the dead. The Gospels describe how Jesus walked on water, fed a crowd of more than 5,000, turned water into wine, and even calmed a storm on a few occasions. The point is that Jesus was no one-trick-pony. He had a very broad and impressive resumé when it came to miracles.

2. There were many witnesses

It's also worth noting just how public Jesus' miracles were. Jesus never had to say, *Guess what I just did!* He didn't do all these miracles when no one was looking or just in front of a few "privileged" followers. His miracles were almost always in the presence of many others. Not only that but on many occasions the eyewitnesses included his sceptical and critical enemies. Pharisees, Sadducees and doubters alike were witnesses to his wonders and lived among those who were healed. They could go on observing those who claimed they had been cured from leprosy or had had their sight restored and verify whether each case was a short-lived hoax or a genuine healing. Put simply, Jesus' miracles were very public and very testable.

Another thing worth mentioning (as was once pointed out to me by a good friend) is that the enemies of Jesus never seemed to deny that he did miraculous things; they just tried to cast them in a negative light. They didn't disagree that Jesus was healing the sick and calming storms; they just attributed his supernatural abilities to demons and not God (Matthew 12 v 24). But no one came forward to accuse Jesus or his followers of being liars in regards to the miracles.

3. There are many details in the accounts

Over the last decade or so, I've had the privilege of taking several trips to Israel—once for a week-long archaeological dig on the shores of Lake Galilee but mostly to act as tour guide for a group of around 35 guests each year. What becomes very apparent to guests is that you can actually pinpoint where a number of the miracles that Jesus performed took place. You can literally stand on the very spot where the Bible claims they occurred—and that's precisely because we're given so many exact details about them in the Gospels. They give us geographical references such as the region or town or village or city which the miracle happened in or near (Capernaum, Bethsaida, Jerusalem or Bethany). Occasionally they tell us the building or road where a certain miracle occurred (at the synagogue or in the temple or on the road to Emmaus, and so on). Likewise, they sometimes give us the specific names of the people who were there, or even the time of year or time of day it happened.

Now, I am not saying that just because you can stand on the alleged location of a miracle 2,000 years later, that proves that it must have happened. But it is compelling that the Gospel writers happily gave such testable pointers to their *contemporaries*. Any of their readers could have easily gone to the village or town in question to check things out for themselves. They could have talked to the eyewitnesses and verified the details.

One of my favourite things to show guests in Israel is the remains of the synagogue in Capernaum on the north shore of Lake Galilee. Capernaum was central to Jesus' ministry in the Gospels, so it's a must-see for historians and pilgrims alike. We are told that the synagogue of Capernaum was where Jesus dramatically healed a man with some kind of a demonic spirit (Mark 1 v 21-28). Most of the structural ruins of the synagogue that you see today are actually from the 4th century, but you can still see the foundational stones of the 1st-century synagogue which was there previously. So you can literally stand where this miracle is supposed to have happened. But that's not my point.

The point is that in Jesus' day, Capernaum was a pretty small village with *only one synagogue* and the Gospel writers knew that. So it's highly significant that Mark tells us that Jesus healed the man in *the* synagogue—not *a* synagogue—in Capernaum. That enabled the people of the day to pinpoint the exact site of the miracle. It's virtually the equivalent of getting the exact GPS co-ordinates of the miracle. Furthermore, we're told that the miracle happened during a service on the Sabbath (the Saturday) when the whole town was shut down and the synagogue would have been packed with many witnesses. And this is just one example of many.

This is why these kinds of details are significant: if that story was circulating in and around Capernaum for three decades, and then was finally written down in Mark's Gospel the 60s AD, it means that anyone hearing or reading that story at the time could have easily gone to *exactly* where it was said to have happened and asked just about anyone in town whether it was true or not. If the Gospel writers knew that the miracle wasn't true, why would they have left themselves wide open to such easy counter-verification?

SEE FOR YOURSELF

Jesus was, and still is, the most famous person who ever lived. Why? Because of what he taught and the way he taught it; and because of what he claimed about himself and the way he backed it up with a consistent life and some impressive miracles.

If you're still sceptical about his miracles, that's understandable. I get that. But I've always felt that there is still enough substantial evidence to at least warrant further investigation, and there's too much for sceptics to lose if it's all true. If Jesus really is God incarnate, then what he said about life and death and heaven and hell really matters, and it is certainly worthy of our consideration. If he really did say that he is the way and the truth and the life, and that no one can get to the Father except through him—and if there's even an outside chance that he really was able to back it all up with dozens of public miracles, including his own resurrection—then that is worth exploring at least. So, why not pick up one of the Gospels and see what you think for yourself?

6. Because the death of Jesus is surprisingly very good news for you

"The point of the death of Christ is that Christ took on the sins of the world, so that what we put out did not come back to us."

Bono, U2

On Saturday morning, 29 July 2006, a small plane carrying a group of sky divers took off from an airport near St. Louis in the US state of Missouri. On board were eight people including Kimberley Dear, a 21-year-old woman from Melbourne, Australia. She had travelled to America to help on a summer camp for children with various disabilities, and now, at the end of the trip, she and a friend decided to fulfil a lifelong dream to go skydiving. They were each paired with a skydiving instructor who would jump out of the plane in tandem with them. Kimberley was "buddied-up" with Robert Cook, an experienced instructor who had successfully completed around 1,700 jumps. The girls recorded their day on film, and in one eerie moment before boarding the plane, Kimberley can be seen turning to the camera and pointing to Robert, saying, "This is the man that's going to save my life". Little did she know what would happen next.

Soon after take-off, the plane got into trouble. Witnesses on the ground said they heard a loud bang and could see smoke coming from the plane's engine. On board, excitement quickly turned to terror. The plane was too low for them to jump out safely with their parachutes, but Robert's experience and training quickly kicked in. He calmly turned to Kimberley and told her that the plane was going to crash and that she should lie on top of him. He told her that he would cradle her in his arms and absorb the impact in his own body as the plane hit the ground. So, through tears, Kimberley did as Robert instructed, and clung on to this man whom she had only met that morning, hoping her life would be spared.

Just seconds later, the plane crashed in an urban area, narrowly missing a number of houses. Robert died instantly, but Kimberley survived. She suffered spinal injuries, a broken pelvis and a range of other minor injuries, but Robert's body had cushioned the impact enough to save Kimberley's life at the expense of his own. In 2008 Robert Cook was posthumously awarded the Star of Courage, Australia's second highest award for bravery.

It's stories like this that remind me of the significance of the death of Christ. The central claim of Christianity—and of Jesus himself—is that he came to rescue us by throwing his own life in harm's way. Similar to Robert Cook, he sacrificed his own life but to cushion us from eternal death. Let me explain...

THE GREAT PROBLEM

As I outlined in chapter 4, crucial to the Christian message is the idea that the world is messed up because we've all grossly ignored God, rebelled against him and walked away from him—in other words, we've all sinned. However, most people these days don't think of sin in these terms.

At one end of the spectrum, some people see sin as just being a bit naughty or mischievous. To them, sin is having a little too much chocolate or being a bit thoughtless. "We're all sinners," they would say, "but it's nothing to be too ashamed of—after all, we're only human". At the other end of the spectrum, others believe that sin only involves the big things like murder or adultery, and if you haven't done those things, then you've got nothing to worry about when you approach the pearly gates.

The Bible, however, teaches something altogether different. It's not just that we've broken a few draconian laws or haven't been religious enough; it's that we've all effectively slapped God in the face and declared war against him.

Jesus graphically illustrated this in one of his most famous stories. It begins with a wealthy father who has two sons. The younger is keen to leave the family household, get as far away as possible and do things his own way. So, one day he comes to his father and asks to be given his inheritance that very instant. Surprisingly, the father graciously divides up the estate and gives the younger son his share. We're told that he promptly heads off to a distant land and squanders his wealth in "wild living"—which, we later find out, includes hiring prostitutes. Soon enough he runs out of money and ends up working in a pig pen, salivating over the slop that the pigs are eating.

You might, at this point, think that the great sin of this rebellious son was his "wild living". But that's not what Jesus and his 1st-century readers would have understood. Yes, the wild living would have brought shame on him and his family, but the great crime was what had happened earlier.

Here was a young man who essentially wanted all the good things that his father could provide for him, but without the father himself. In reality, he wanted his father dead, or at least out of the way. But as soon as the young lad could do what he liked, it all went horribly wrong.

This is only half the parable, but it's the part of the story that I want us to dwell on. Every single one of us has done spiritually what that son did in the parable. We've all in our heart of hearts wanted the gifts that God has given us without God "in the way". Each of us has taken and used this world and our lives as we want to, but we have ignored God and pushed him aside. The result is that we're now living in a world where things have all gone horribly wrong—a world full of disorder, crime, suffering and death. Furthermore, we have deeply *wronged* God by rejecting his good plans for us. And we now stand guilty before him. None of us deserve his blessings, his gifts or his friendship.

Put simply, we deserve his anger, not his love.

HOW CAN A GOD OF LOVE BE ANGRY?

Many of us these days are often disturbed by the idea of a God who is wrathful or angry. Most of my non-Christian friends find this particularly hard to accept. Even a few Christians I know are uncomfortable with it.

I clearly remember being in a lecture in the first year of my theological degree when we were studying a particularly disturbing and graphic part of the Old Testament that spoke of God's anger with the sinful Israelites. There came a point in the lecture when a student shot up his hand and asked, "How can a loving God be so full of wrath and anger?" He was asking what many of the rest of us were thinking, so we all hung on the lecturer's answer. He slowly lowered his glasses, smiled and then said something along these lines:

"Many of us have a real problem with an angry, vengeful God because we live in the developed countries of the West. In the affluent West we tend not to see pain and suffering and injustice on the scale that others do in some parts the world. In some parts of the world, life is so difficult because of an

awful dictator, a brutal war or a corrupt government. And in situations like that, just about all that people long for and pray for is justice. Their prayers aren't about passing an exam or hoping that God would stop the turbulence on an airplane. They're pleading for God to bring about justice. To them, a loving God is a God who deals out justice and is not indifferent to crime, war and sin. For them, a God who cares and a God who is willing do something about the injustice that they and their ancestors have faced is a very comforting thought. So, Scriptures like this, which speak of a God who is willing to bring wicked people to account, are enormously reassuring to them. We often miss this in the West because the call for justice is not nearly as strong."

I clearly remember being struck by that answer. Since then, my wife and I have been to countries in Asia and the Middle East where we have met people whose lives have been torn apart by a ruthless government or a senseless war or extreme poverty. Since 2003 my wife has participated in dozens of missions with the World Health Organisation (WHO) and has witnessed first-hand unbearable poverty. In 2016 she was in West Africa working to help stop the spread of Ebola. The poverty she saw not only saddened her but deeply angered her. These experiences have given us both a glimpse into why God might be angry and why actually we all deserve his wrath.

THE GREAT SOLUTION

The Bible talks unblushingly about our guilt and God's anger—but it doesn't stop there. It also talks about God's *amazing grace*. God, thankfully, is graciously willing to forgive each and every one of us, and all at his expense! He was willing to come in the person of Christ and, on that Roman cross, bear the consequences of all our wrongdoing and shame. *The main message of Christianity is that God came in human form ultimately to be a substitute for us.* On the cross, all our debt, punishment and shame was set upon Christ, allowing us to be fully exempt. Christ came to cushion the blow that we all really deserve. In effect, he laid down his own life to save ours: not just one life for another, but his life for any of us who are willing to be "cushioned" by him.

In a series of very revealing interviews with the French music journalist Michka Assayas, the philanthropist and musician Bono—frontman of U2—was asked about his faith in Jesus. At a particularly poignant moment during one of the interviews Assayas quipped, "'The Son of God who takes away the sins of the world.' I wish I could believe that." Bono responded:

"I love the idea of the sacrificial Lamb. I love the idea that God says, Look ... there are certain results to the way we are, to selfishness, and there's a mortality as part of your very sinful nature, and, let's face it, you're not living a very good life, are you? There are consequences to actions. The point of the death of Christ is that Christ took on the sins of the world, so that what we put out did not come back to us, and that our sinful nature does not reap the obvious death. That's the point. It should keep us humbled."[14]

THE GREAT SWAP

A number of years ago now, a minister I know in Sydney was charged with the responsibility of reaching the young men and women who were training to be tradespeople at the city's colleges (plumbers, carpenters, electricians and so on). He and his team came up with a slogan that captured the essence of the message of Christianity:

"Jesus did a trade... His life for yours!"

Jesus came to do a swap: his life for yours. As this is such a central theme of the Bible, it shouldn't surprise us that the whole idea is conveyed in a myriad of wonderful ways throughout its pages. There are many passages we could draw on. One of my favourites, and perhaps one of the most powerful, is the story of Barabbas. The story is so illustrative of the essence of Christianity that it's narrated for us in all four Gospels.

Barabbas was a Jewish rebel, in prison at the very time when Jesus was arrested and tried. Barabbas seems to have been arrested for instigating and carrying out crimes against the Roman occupiers, the very thing that Jesus was being accused of. Both of them faced execution on the orders of Pontius Pilate, the Roman governor, who was in charge of ensuring Roman imperial rule over Judea and its Jewish capital, Jerusalem.

The point is that Barabbas was clearly guilty and Jesus was totally innocent. Interestingly, Pilate, who held the fate of both men, knew this too. He knew that Jesus was totally innocent of the charges against him and that Barabbas was a notorious troublemaker—a Zealot—and was viciously opposed to Roman rule.[15] But, because there were so many powerful people who wanted Jesus dead, Pilate was in too weak a position to release him on his own authority. Instead, he tried to pull one last string to have Jesus released without having to take the responsibility himself.

The day of Jesus' arrest and trial was the day before the Jewish festival of Passover. This was (and still is) a very special time for Jewish people. It was one of the three times in the year when Jewish pilgrims came from all over the Roman Empire to Jerusalem to celebrate a highly significant moment in Israel's history: their miraculous escape from Egypt, led by Moses, over 1,200 years before. The exodus began after the plague of death passed through the land of Egypt but "passed over" the homes of the Israelites, who had sacrificed an animal and smeared the blood on their door posts. The sacrificial lambs enabled the Israelites to flee to the promised land.

By Jesus' day, the Jews were once again under the thumb of an enemy power: the Romans. The annual Passover celebration was a time when national pride was at boiling point, and the population of Jerusalem swelled to up to six times its normal size. Consequently, the city was often on the edge of rioting each year. In fact, this was the very reason why Pontius Pilate was in Jerusalem. Most of the year Pilate resided in Caesarea, a much nicer harbour city that lay 60 miles north-west of Jerusalem on the Mediterranean coast. He was generally only ever in Jerusalem on these sorts of occasions, to make sure that things didn't get out of hand.

Each year, in order to keep things peaceful between the Jews and the Romans, the Roman governor would release a Jewish prisoner selected by the Jews, as a goodwill gesture. On this occasion, Pilate marshalled Barabbas and Jesus to be the two candidates for release. The scene at this point is very famous and features in just about any film on the life of Jesus. It's also been depicted many times in the paintings of a number of well-known artists, such as Antonio Ciseri's "Behold the Man".

The crowd were asked which prisoner should be released. They yelled out, "Give us Barabbas". As for Jesus, they cried out, "Crucify him!" Pilate was forced to play the hand he didn't want to play. Barabbas was released, and Jesus was led away to be crucified.

It's an astounding illustration of what Good Friday and the crucifixion of Jesus is really all about. Barabbas represents you and me. We, the guilty ones, go free, while Jesus, the innocent one, was taken away to be punished and die. Yet this was the plan all along. It was the gracious plan of God in a nutshell, and it's good news for any of us when we accept it for ourselves.

Incidentally, Pietro Sarubbi, the Italian actor who played Barabbas in the film *The Passion of Christ*, directed by Mel Gibson, became a Christian through the filming of this very scene. Sarubbi was specifically instructed by Gibson not to look at Jesus (played by Jim Caviezel) until the very moment of filming. Finally, when the moment came, with both actors in full costume and the cameras rolling, Sarubbi as Barabbas finally looked across at Caviezel playing Jesus. At that moment Sarubbi was literally stunned. Caviezel was drenched in artificial blood and almost unrecognisable—his make-up portraying the disfigurement from the beatings that Christ would have suffered—standing motionless and staring back at Sarubbi. Sarubbi was completely taken aback by the earnest and compassionate look Caviezel gave him.

At that moment, on set, the significance of the scene they were recreating dawned on him. Jesus the innocent one was swapping places with him, the guilty one. Barabbas would be freed; Jesus would die. The moment was so life-transforming for Sarubbi that he wrote a book about the experience entitled *Da Barabba a Gesù. Convertito da uno sguardo (From Barabbas to Jesus: Converted by a Glance)*.[16]

THE GREAT SENTENCE

Let me sign off this chapter by getting you to look at one of the most famous Bible verses of all. Even if you haven't read a Bible or been to church, you may have heard of this verse:

For God so loved the world that he gave his one and only Son, that whoever believes in him shall not perish but have eternal life. (John 3 v 16)

It's a popular verse because it's basically the message of the Bible in a single sentence.

It's telling us that there is a God and that this God loves the world, despite the fact that the world is so unlovable. God loves this world, including you and me, despite our greed, self-centredness, pride, and rejection of him. In fact, he loves us so much that he gave over his Son. The word "Son" doesn't mean that Jesus was God's biological son—both the Father and the Son have existed for eternity. But it does speak of the closeness between them, and the fact that Jesus was the full representative of the "Father". He was God in human form.

Jesus Christ was "given" over as a sacrifice to be a substitute in our place. But, as we know from dozens of other verses in the Bible, Jesus wasn't an unwilling participant. He knew this was his mission, and he wanted to do it, even though he wrestled with the pain of it all. We may therefore also say that Jesus *gave himself* over to die. He willingly took on the role of being the sacrificial lamb for us as he swapped his life for ours and, in doing so, was able to solve the great problem of the world and reconcile us to God. This means that "whoever believes" in Jesus—whoever accepts this swap for themselves—receives God's forgiveness and is promised eternal life beyond the grave instead of the judgment of eternal death.

I read once of a little girl who decided to write out the words of John 3 v 16 in big letters for a poster to be hung on her bedroom wall. However, she misread the verse and inadvertently blended two of the words together. So instead of writing, "For God so loved the world", she wrote, "For God solved the world". When her mother saw it, she immediately noticed that her daughter had made a mistake. But as she reflected on it, she decided that her daughter's version was worth keeping. Jesus had come to solve the world's great problem.

Now if all of this is really true—if Jesus really was God in human form, if he really did come here to swap places with us, if his death on that Roman cross really did pay for all our wrongdoing, and if pledging our allegiance to him and believing in who he is and what he's done secures your salvation—then that is an offer definitely worth (re)considering.

7. Because if Jesus really did rise from the dead, then it would confirm everything

"If Jesus rose from the dead, then you have to accept all that he said; if he didn't rise from the dead, then why worry about any of what he said? The issue on which everything hangs is not whether or not you like his teaching but whether or not he rose from the dead."

Timothy Keller, *The Reason for God*

Let's, just for a moment, entertain a thought together: if Jesus *really* did die on that Roman cross—if he *really* was completely and utterly dead, kaput, finished, gone, deceased—but then he *really* did come back to life and gave overwhelming proof that he was truly resurrected from the dead... you would have to admit that would have some pretty major implications.

We'll get to the question of *whether* Jesus rose from the dead later in the chapter. But before we do, it's worth thinking through what it would mean *if* he did. If Jesus truly rose from the dead, then this was not only arguably the most significant event in history. It would also go a long way towards validating who he was, what he said and what he claimed he had done.

IT WOULD CONFIRM WHO HE IS

For three years before his death, Jesus had been showing and subtly telling the disciples that he was God incarnate—God in human form—but it wasn't until the resurrection that the penny fully dropped for his followers. His resurrection totally confirmed for them that Jesus was who he said he was and, from the moment they saw him alive again, they confidently affirmed his divinity. In fact, as soon as the disciple Thomas saw Jesus alive again, he said to him, "My Lord and my God!" (John 20 v 28). No disciple had ever said that previously. The resurrection was arguably the turning point for the first followers of Jesus.

Whether you live in the 1st century or 21st century, if true, the resurrection demonstrates that Jesus was no ordinary man. In medical science, conquering death is regarded as the final frontier. Every one of us dies. No one can ultimately stop it, cure it or reverse it; despite our greatest efforts. So, for someone to be able to conquer death would mean they had some kind of super-natural powers and were in a totally different category to everyone that has ever lived. If Jesus did rise from the dead, then it would go a long way to defending the case that he is the Son of God.

IT WOULD CONFIRM WHAT HE SAID

Likewise, if Jesus really did rise from the dead, it would also seem to confirm what he said about God, life, death and life beyond the grave. If you were listening to a person giving a talk on mountaineering, it would make a big difference if you knew they had just returned from climbing Mount Everest. Or if someone was offering to be your swimming coach, I'm sure you'd be much more willing to take their advice if you knew they had previously won a gold medal at the Olympic Games. Likewise, if Jesus rose from the dead, it gives a lot more weight to his claim that he came to bring us life and life to the full (John 10 v 10). To say that you are "the resurrection and the life" (John 11 v 25) sounds pretty arrogant, but to back it up by resurrecting yourself puts things into an entirely new perspective.

It's also worth pointing out that on several occasions Jesus actually predicted his resurrection. He told the disciples that he would be arrested, killed (by crucifixion) and rise again three days later (Mark 8 v 31; 9 v 31; 10 v 33-34). The fact that what he predicted came true shows that what he says is trustworthy.

IT WOULD CONFIRM WHAT HE DID

If Jesus really physically rose from the grave that first Easter Sunday, then it confirms the significance of his death on Good Friday.

The core teaching of Christianity is that Jesus died on the cross in order to take upon himself the sins of the world, thus enabling mankind to have a fresh start and an eternal relationship with God. However, without the resurrection, Jesus would just have been a mere mortal man/prophet/teacher or whatever. His death wouldn't have been sufficient for the rest of us; he would simply be, at best, a religious martyr.

The writers of the New Testament recognised this. Writing to the early Greek converts in the city of Corinth (who were struggling with the idea of bodily resurrection), the apostle Paul basically said that if Jesus hadn't risen from the dead, the Christian faith was "useless" (1 Corinthians 15 v 14). Similarly, writing around a decade later, the apostle Peter began his first New Testament letter by saying that the saving work of Jesus' death on the cross is all tied up in the hope of the resurrection (1 Peter 1 v 3-5).

Without the resurrection, Christianity falls completely flat. If Jesus lay in the grave, his death was no more important than that of any other martyr. However, if the resurrection is true, it confirms that Christ's death on the cross really did pay for the sins of his people and accomplish forgiveness for all those who believe in him.

IT WOULD CONFIRM WHAT WILL HAPPEN

Finally, if Jesus really did rise from the dead, it would confirm what he and the apostles said about the future. Speaking personally, much of my Christian hope for life beyond the grave is based on the past resurrection of Jesus. Let me explain.

At its core, much of the teaching of Jesus and his apostles (and the whole Bible for that matter) is about the dawning of a new age: a total reboot of the world and humanity that has begun with Jesus' own ministry. What we see in Jesus' ministry, narrated for us in the New Testament, is both the beginning of this and a glimpse of things to come. In many ways, his miracles in particular are like the preview of a film—a "peek through a window" into what life is going to be like in God's kingdom, which is still yet to come fully. This is *especially* true of Jesus' resurrection. Writing to communities that were very familiar with farming, the apostle Paul describes Jesus' resurrection as being like the "firstfruits" of a harvest to come (1 Corinthians 15 v 20). Or, as the 20th-century author C.S. Lewis put it:

"[Jesus] is the … 'the pioneer of life'. He has forced open a door that has been locked since the death of the first man."[17]

For Christians, then, the first Easter Sunday wasn't just the first day of another week; rather, it was the first day of a whole new era.

The first Christians didn't simply teach that once a believer dies, they go off to a cloudy, ethereal existence called "heaven". Rather, they taught that one day all Christians will be *physically* raised to life, with a newly constructed body, to live in a new physical world. It is Jesus' own bodily resurrection that gives the believer a guarantee of their own bodily resurrection in the future.

Again, if Jesus didn't rise from the dead, then all this talk of a "new age" and things to come would be just mere words and wishful thinking. By default, Jesus would simply be just another prophet or teacher, or perhaps worse! But if the bodily resurrection of Christ has really occurred, then it authenticates what he said about the future. It means that natural sceptics like me can have great confidence that our own bodies will be resurrected one day to enjoy life in God's new world.

DID IT REALLY HAPPEN?

So, the question we must all consider then is this: did Jesus really rise from the dead? Was it "real news" or "fake news"? Is there any evidence? Can you believe in the resurrection with intellectual integrity?

Well, as I begin to attempt to answer these questions, there's a couple of things I would first like you to be aware of.

1. There's a lot of scholarly material on the resurrection

First of all, there is a truckload of detailed, serious scholarship on the subject. Much of it, I'm sure, would put most people to sleep, but it's worth knowing that Jesus' resurrection and the subsequent rise of early Christianity has generated a lot of high-quality research in the scholarly world. Perhaps none is more impressive than N .T. Wright's book on the resurrection: *The Resurrection of the Son of God*. My copy is around 800 pages long and has caused one of the bookshelves in my study to sag! That's because it's a very thorough, historical and theological assessment of the resurrection—and by no means the only one in its field.

2. The New Testament accounts are historical documents

Second, the accounts of Jesus' death and resurrection in the New Testament are considered by historians as valid, historical documents, equal to any other such sources from the ancient world. Scholars don't disregard the New Testament just because it's a collection of religious documents and therefore "biased".

All historians acknowledge that any document we have (whether ancient or modern) is written with at least some kind of agenda or bias to it. For example, one of the best historical sources we have on Alexander the Great comes from the ancient biographer Plutarch, who penned his biography on the famous Greek Macedonian general around 400 years later. Plutarch was clearly a fan of Alexander and either ignores or glosses over many of Alexander's moral failures.[18] However, no historian of Alexander disregards the writings of Plutarch simply because he wrote with a favourable bias. They just take that into account when assessing his work, as they do when assessing any historical document. The fact of the matter is that scholars of history know that virtually no document was ever written from a position of total neutrality.

Hence, the resurrection of Jesus isn't just a topic of interest for Christian scholars. Many of our best historians, past and present, who study the accounts of the resurrection on a serious level, are sceptics or people from other faiths.[19] Those historians might not come to the same conclusion that the New Testament authors come to about Jesus and the resurrection (although some do), but they still regard these ancient Christian sources as historical evidence and the resurrection as a subject of great importance.

Now, back to answering our question: did it really happen?

Well, of course I can't give you conclusive, watertight proof that Jesus rose from the dead. I wish I could. But here are several things that help me to believe in the resurrection and to stay devoted to the Christian faith, and I'd love you too to consider these.

3. All the evidence we currently have points to a bodily resurrection, not away from it

When you survey the historical sources that we have on Jesus' resurrection (whether Christian, Jewish or Roman), they all at least point in the direction of a real resurrection. I'm not saying that all the historical evidence we have on the subject *proves* the resurrection, but it certainly stacks up *in favour* of it.

Think of it this way. In a missing person's case, a detective might start with several possibilities regarding what could have happened:

- The missing person might still be alive somewhere and they're hiding for some reason.

- Or, they might have secretly committed suicide somewhere.

- Or, the person has been murdered and the body is buried somewhere.

- Or, they went on holiday and forgot to tell anyone about it.

The detective would then look at all the evidence carefully and see where the trail of evidence points, and then come to the best conclusion. They might not be able to *prove* their final conclusion, but they can at least say, "Based on the evidence, this is what is most likely to have happened".

In part, historians are like detectives, trying to assess all the evidence so that they can piece together what happened in the past. In the same way, we may have several initial theories about what might have happened to Jesus:

- Jesus didn't die but simply "passed out" on the cross and then revived in the tomb, and subsequently fooled the disciples into thinking he was raised from the dead.

- Or, the disciples stole the body and made the whole thing up.

- Or, perhaps the disciples never intended their accounts to be taken literally. What they actually meant was that Jesus "rose in their hearts" spiritually.

- Or, Jesus really did rise from the dead.

Like a good detective, the good historian looks at all the evidence of any historical event, tries to divest themselves of any bias or prejudices, and sees where the evidence leads them. What I can quite confidently tell you is that many of the best historians on the resurrection have ended up concluding that all the evidence points in the direction of a bodily resurrection, or at least that *the first followers of Jesus had a very strong conviction that Jesus rose bodily from the grave.*

Again, I'm not arguing that all these historians say that the evidence *proves* the resurrection, but many seem to concede that the trail of evidence leans in that direction.

Another book in my study is by Professor Ed Sanders, formerly of Duke University, North Carolina, and a world-renowned scholar on the historical Jesus. In the final chapter of his book *The Historical Figure of Jesus*, Sanders concludes:

"That Jesus' followers (and later Paul) had resurrection experiences is, in my judgment, a fact. What the reality was that gave rise to the experiences I do not know."[20]

Likewise, in the penultimate chapter of his tome on the resurrection (mentioned above), N.T. Wright says:

"The proposal that Jesus was bodily raised from the dead possesses unrivalled power to explain the historical data at the heart of early Christianity."[21]

CONSIDERING THE EVIDENCE

So, what evidence do we have and in what way does it point to a bodily resurrection? Here are several more things I'd like you to consider.

1. Jesus was crucified

Almost all our sources on Jesus' death (both Christian and non-Christian) tell us that he was executed on a cross. This is significant—most obviously because, if Jesus didn't really die, then he couldn't have risen from the dead. However, we can have great confidence that Jesus did really die precisely because he was *crucified*. We might have a lot more reason to doubt Jesus' death, and therefore his resurrection, if indeed Jesus was lost at sea or fell over a cliff or was murdered in secret. However, a very public execution by a professional execution squad makes Jesus' death a certainty.

Several decades ago, a few sceptics called into question Jesus' death by crucifixion because it was believed that crucifixion was rare at the time and that Jewish people in particular weren't crucified but only ever stoned. However, these days the overwhelming scholarly consensus is that not only was crucifixion common at the time of Jesus but that Jews were some of the *most frequently crucified people* in the Roman Empire! One of the world's most eminent ancient historians is Robin Lane Fox: a prolific writer and a giant in his field. In his highly readable book on ancient Greece and Rome he categorically states, "Whatever the truth of the first Easter, the crucifixion, at least, is a historical fact".[22] In fact, historian Paula Fredriksen of Boston University has declared that "the crucifixion is the strongest single fact we have about Jesus".[23]

More to the point, crucifixion was almost always done publicly and by a team of professionals whose job it was to ensure the death of the victim. I don't want to get into the gory details but it was virtually physically impossible to crucify someone on your own; you needed a team of people to do it, and there was usually a head executioner overseeing it all. This is what we're told happened in Jesus' case (John 19 v 23; Luke 23 v 47).[24]

Also, we are told by the Gospel writer John (who witnessed the crucifixion for himself) that Jesus was stabbed in the side with a spear by one of the Roman soldiers to confirm that he had indeed died (John 19 v 34-35). Furthermore, before releasing Jesus to be buried, the soldiers would have had to have handled the body and the centurion would have needed to confirm first-hand that Jesus had indeed died. That was their job. Presumably, then, they would have checked the body for any signs of life, and if Christ was dead, they would have seen *pallor mortis* (the skin becoming pale) and felt *algor mortis* (the body growing cold). They wouldn't have surrendered the body to be buried if they had thought the victim was still alive.

The evidence, then, in no way supports the theory that Jesus "swooned" (fainted, passed out) on the cross, was removed while still alive, and revived in the tomb shortly thereafter. That not only runs against all the written testimony but also contrary to what we know about Roman crucifixion and the imperial execution protocol.

2. All agree that the tomb was empty

From all our available sources, it seems that everyone agreed that the tomb that Jesus had been placed in on the Friday was empty by the Sunday. No one suggested that the women, who went first, and the apostles, who arrived afterward, went to the wrong tomb. The initial question among both Jesus' disciples and his enemies was "How did the tomb become empty?" No one, it seems, questioned the fact of the empty tomb; they just debated how it got that way.

If there was any possibility that the followers of Jesus had got their GPS co-ordinates wrong, it is curious that not one of our sources reveals that someone then suggested going to the "right" tomb. If the disciples had gone to the wrong grave, any one of Jesus' enemies could have gone to the correct one and have simply produced the corpse. However, no one did.

3. The resurrection was part of the preaching of the first disciples

Of great note to historians is that the bodily resurrection of Jesus was never confined to the margins of the preaching and letters of the first generation of Christians. The resurrection, from the very beginning of Christianity, was part of its core teachings. Despite what you might have read or heard from some of the New Atheists in recent years, the resurrection wasn't a much-later addition to the Christian message, fabricated by church leaders further down the track. It was at the centre of the good news from the very start.

In the last 50 years or so, a lot of work has gone into discerning what the core teachings of the earliest Christians were prior to the finished forms we have of the Gospels and letters of the New Testament. Our earliest sources on Jesus are actually the letters of the apostle Paul. All of his 13 letters in the New Testament pre-date the four Gospels, so they are a goldmine for historians and theologians alike. All of them were written within 35 years of Jesus' crucifixion and each of them in one way or another refers to the resurrection. But beyond that, within these letters scholars can detect early Christian sayings and creeds, and possibly even songs that were taught from the first decades of the Christian era (such as 1 Corinthians 15 v 3-7, Philippians 2 v 6-11, and Colossians 1 v 15-20). Each of these early Christian summaries within Paul's letters contains references to the resurrection.

As New Testament historian and former Bishop of North Sydney Paul Barnett states:

"The heart of the apostles' message was the resurrection of Jesus. Whether it was Peter preaching to Jews in Jerusalem or Paul preaching to Gentiles in Athens, their announcement focused on the resurrection of Jesus from the dead. The focal

*point of the New Testament and of Christianity is, in Paul's
words, 'Jesus Christ, risen from the dead.'"*[25]

Others argue that while the resurrection was indeed part
of the first message of the early Christians, what these first
believers really meant by "resurrection" wasn't a bodily
resurrection but a spiritual one—that Jesus "rose in their
hearts". However, that argument among historians in
the know is (if you'll pardon the pun) virtually dead. To
say that the first Christians actually meant to teach that
Jesus rose spiritually, not physically, is almost impossible
to square with just about everything else they say in the
New Testament, especially what they say in the passages
on the resurrection. In no uncertain terms, the Gospels
and several of the New Testament letters tell us that the
disciples spoke with the risen Jesus, touched him and
ate with him in specific locations, and on one occasion
in the presence of up to 500 people. In fact, rather than
saying that Jesus simply rose spiritually in their hearts,
it seems that the authors of the New Testament bent
over backwards to say the very opposite—that Jesus'
resurrection was stunningly physical!

On top of that, all the evidence we have from the
opponents of Jesus and Christians tell us that they took it
that the apostles meant a bodily resurrection. Put simply
and rather bluntly, to say that the apostles taught that
Jesus rose spiritually and not bodily from the grave not
only lacks any evidence, but is completely contradictory to
the evidence that we do have.

4. The first city of the Christian message

It is also noteworthy to historians that the news of Jesus' resurrection originated from within Jerusalem. The announcement of "Jesus, risen from the dead" didn't first come from Galilee (75 miles or so to the north) or from further afield, where it could not have been easily verified, but from within the very city where Jesus was supposed to have risen. This meant that whatever the first disciples were saying about Jesus could easily be tried and tested. Sceptics would have been freely able to speak to anyone who witnessed his crucifixion to determine if he really did die; they could have gone to the tomb themselves to confirm that it was indeed empty; they could have spoken to the eyewitnesses of the resurrection and grilled them on their testimony and so on. The fact that the good news about Jesus' death and resurrection arose in the vicinity of where it was said to have happened is very striking.

5. The number of witnesses

Another thing worth pointing out is that our earliest sources on the resurrection tell us that there were many witnesses who saw Jesus alive at different locations. Jesus didn't appear to just a few people on one particular foggy evening after they had had a couple of pints or an overindulgence of strong cheese. We are told that Jesus physically appeared to many (perfectly sober) people in Jerusalem and in Galilee, and that he appeared at these locations on a number of occasions at different times of the day.

The apostle Paul not only happily names a number of these witnesses but also (almost casually) mentions that on at least one of those occasions, Jesus appeared to around "500 people at the same time" (1 Corinthians 15 v 6). While he concedes that some folk within that large group had since died, he also says that many of them were still alive.

Just think about that for a moment. If indeed 500 people really saw Jesus alive, all at the same time, that almost totally rules out the theory that the disciples simply imagined it, or that they were hallucinating the whole thing. It's also worth noting that if many of that group of 500 were still alive, then anyone reading Paul's words could go and find at least some of them and hear their accounts first-hand.

6. The change in and conviction of the disciples

Another undeniable fact that virtually all scholars of history seem to agree on is the radical change that occurred in the disciples. Within a matter of months, the remaining followers of Jesus (a mere 120 of them) went from being a bunch of confused, frightened no-hopers to a confident and courageous group of over 3,000 believers, who boldly and unashamedly proclaimed that Jesus was indeed the Christ, who had died and risen again. It is an undeniable fact that Christianity began to spread like wildfire in and around Jerusalem, and within 30 years it had spread across the Mediterranean to reach the capital of the empire: Rome.

What can explain that? Could mere hearsay or legend generate such conviction and radical change in the disciples? There's no indication that they were motivated by money. The disciples weren't like some notorious tele-evangelists, preaching for financial gain through swindling the poor. In fact, the very opposite was true— they went about preaching at great cost to themselves and their families.

Some critics have suggested that in order to "save face" the disciples concocted the story of the resurrection. But the crucifixion and the resurrection were the very things that got them laughed out of the synagogues and chased out the theatres and market-places of the empire. If the disciples had wanted to save face, they could have done it by simply proclaiming that Jesus was a great teacher and true martyr. But they didn't! It seems that what sparked the transformation and subsequent preaching of the first Christians was a genuine belief that Jesus was who he really claimed to be, that his death truly did pay for the sins of the world and that he really did rise from the dead.

7. The deaths of the disciples

All this leads me to the death of the disciples. It's incredibly significant to me, and to many Christians I know, that the disciples not only proclaimed that they'd seen and met the risen Jesus but that they went to the grave affirming it without recanting. To the very end, the disciples didn't waver from insisting that they had seen, heard, met, touched and even eaten with Jesus after he was crucified and buried. Admittedly the sources are a little hazy, but the general consensus is that out of the eleven remaining disciples (since Judas, who betrayed Jesus, had committed suicide), ten of them were martyred for their claim that Jesus was the Son of God and that he had risen bodily from the dead. (The apostle John was the only one to die a natural death.) Why didn't the apostles recant under threat of execution? Why would they die for something they *knew* was a lie? That doesn't make sense.

Not only that, but they were killed using some of the most brutal of methods of torture and execution of antiquity—including crucifixion. I've just been thumbing my way through what may be the most extensive study (to date) on crucifixion in the ancient world: *Crucifixion in the Mediterranean World* by John Granger Cook. Its 450 pages cover everything we know about crucifixion from the Persians to the Punics, and from the Greeks to the Romans. It is a fascinating but pretty grim read. I probably don't need to tell you this, but crucifixion, in its various forms, was truly, unbelievably, awfully horrid. It's no accident that our word "excruciating" comes from the word "crucifixion".

How did ancient people view death by crucifixion? One of the most striking insights for us comes from Seneca, the Roman philosopher and statesman, and a contemporary of Jesus and the apostles.

"Can anyone be found who would prefer wasting away in pain, dying limb by limb, or letting out his life drop by

drop, rather than expiring once for all? Can any man be found willing to be fastened to the accursed tree, long sickly, already deformed, swelling with ugly wounds on shoulders and chest, and drawing the breath of life amid long drawn-out agony? He would have many excuses for dying even before mounting the cross."[26]

It's compelling, then, that when some of the disciples were threatened with crucifixion, they didn't recant. The apostle Peter was one of them, crucified upside down on an inverted cross in Rome. Despite all the terrifying pain that awaited them, they wouldn't deny their testimony that Jesus was the Son of God and that he indeed rose from the dead.

ASSESSING THE EVIDENCE

My point is this: when, like good detectives, we look at all the evidence and assess all the sources on the resurrection of Jesus, it seems to point in the direction of a bodily resurrection. Other theories—that the disciples made it up, or that they originally meant that Jesus simply rose spiritually, or that the women went to the wrong tomb—have no major evidence supporting them and actually end up contradicting the evidence we *do* have. As one lawyer has put it, "The silence of history is deafening when it comes to the testimony *against* the resurrection".[27]

Many years ago, I was a leader on a teen church camp in Australia. We had taken about 30 teenagers to a low-budget activity centre about 2 hours south-west of

Sydney for a weekend of games and sport and a series of talks.

On the first night, immediately after lights out, I retired to the room I was sharing with another leader when, all of a sudden, we heard an almighty BANG that clearly came from the adjacent boys' dorm. We both looked at each other in shock and simultaneously said, "What the heck was that?!" We ran into the dorm and turned on all the lights. In the middle of the room were two dishevelled boys, both standing with guilty faces. The room was a mess and their pyjamas were ripped. They had clearly been wrestling and we had caught them in the act. It wasn't too much of a surprise, though, as these rather likeable lads were the most mischievous of the group.

"What was that noise?" I asked.

"What noise?" they replied with cheeky grins.

"What was that loud bang?"

"What bang?"

The conversation went to and fro like that for a few minutes, before we noticed that directly behind the boys was a huge dent in the plaster wall. It was virtually the shape of one of them!

"Did you do that?" we asked.

"Nope," came the quick reply.

We asked them again, but they kept denying that they

had had anything to do with it. We sent them to bed and went away to work out what we'd tell the camp owners. It was clear to us that these lads were responsible; we just couldn't prove it. All the evidence was there: the sound of the bang, the two of them standing there with their clothes ripped, the character of the suspects, the size and shape of the dent in the wall, and so on. We couldn't ultimately *prove* that these lads had done it, but all the data certainly *pointed that way*.

In a similar way, I can't conclusively prove that Jesus rose from the dead. No one can.

But what I can say is this: just about all historians seem to agree that around 2,000 years ago, there was a massive BANG, and the sound of it has reverberated and echoed down through two millennia. When we go and investigate what the noise might have been and look at all the evidence, there is a large historical dent in the 1st century—and it's the outline of a resurrected man.

P.S. Why I've (re)considered Christianity

In June 2019, around the time I started to piece this book together, I received some life-changing news. I was told I had a cancer.

A few months earlier I had had what I thought was just a simple toothache. Being an overconfident male, I thought I could see it off through sheer willpower, and so I just ignored it. (Besides, like most of us, I didn't like going to the dentist.) But soon the pain escalated, and I reluctantly went to my local dentist to discuss having my wisdom teeth seen to.

However, before I could undergo any treatment, the pain began to get the better of me. My jaw and cheek had begun to swell so much that I started to look like a chipmunk with a mouthful of nuts. My wife rushed me to the hospital where she works as one of the directors, and within 24 hours I was under a general anaesthetic, having the offending wisdom tooth removed.

I awoke the following morning to a semicircle of smiling doctors and medical students at the bottom of my bed, and it was then that one of them told me that they had discovered a cyst under the offending tooth and it was penetrating the jaw bone. They happily informed me that they had successfully removed the cyst, but they still needed to do some tests on it to see if it was benign or not. Since I was a healthy and relatively "young" guy, they were confident that it was unlikely to be cancerous, so I thought little of it. That is, until I was called back to the hospital a week later to discuss the results.

I can clearly remember hearing those life-changing words as I sat in the doctor's surgery: "We've got your results back. I'm sorry to tell you Mr. Shaw but you have cancer." I was totally stunned. Immediately my vision began to narrow, as if I was looking through a pair of cheap binoculars. As the doctor continued, my ears began to fail too. Just like in the movies, everything was starting to go weird. The doctor calmly went on to tell me that they were going to have to remove at least a third of my jaw and use bone from the fibula in my right leg to reconstruct my face. Now the whole room began to spin, and even though I was seated, I had to ask the doctor if I could lie down; the news was starting to make me pass out.

Less than two weeks later I had a total of 19 hours of surgery and spent just over a fortnight in hospital. The surgery seemed to be a success, and by the start of 2020 I was beginning to feel and look like my old self again. That is, until I started to have trouble closing my left eye. While on holiday in Uruguay, my left eyelid became paralysed. As hard as I tried, I couldn't close it. When I blinked, it was only the right eye that shut. When we returned to London, I had a few tests and was told that the cancer had returned.

In April 2020 I underwent six weeks of intense radiotherapy, a treatment that required a hospital visit five days a week. At the end of those gruelling weeks, I was then given the devastating news that the radiotherapy hadn't worked; the tumour was still growing, and now I was in real trouble.

As I write this, I'm currently three months into having immunotherapy. It's really the last thing the medical world can throw at my cancer. Even if it works well, it's highly likely that my life will be considerably shortened. I'm yet to find out whether the treatment is working or not.

I'm telling you all this for one reason: I too have had to reconsider Christianity. Having death on my very own doorstep has forced me to do a serious reassessment of my faith, including everything I've said in this book. Do I really believe this stuff? Is it all just wishful thinking? Is there a God, and when I die (maybe soon), will I really go to a utopian paradise of bliss and tranquillity that we call heaven? Did Jesus really say and do all those things that the Bible claims? And did he really die for me and rise from the dead a few days later?

In short, my cancer has forced me to reconsider the integrity and credibility of my beliefs.

Yet in the end, far from having been shaken, I can honestly tell you that having this life-threatening illness has actually sharpened and increased my faith. As I stare at the possibility of an early death, I am, in fact, more confident than ever in these things. This book isn't just an academic argument for me; it's a very sincere and personal one. Everything in it is written from a deep, road-tested conviction that this stuff matters more than anything else in the world—for me and for you. With this in mind, I really do hope you (re)consider Christianity for yourself.

What next?

In one of the last scenes in *The Shawshank Redemption*, one of the main characters, Red, is finally released from prison and makes his way to the foot of an obscure oak tree in a hayfield in Buxton, Maine, where he finds a metal box and letter hidden for him written by his good friend and fellow inmate Andy Dufresne. The letter begins, "Dear Red... If you've come this far, maybe you're willing to come a little further?"

So if, after (re)considering the content of this book, you're willing to come a little further, then may I suggest one or all of the following:

- Find a committed, knowledgeable Christian and continue to ask them questions. Hopefully they'll find the time for you and help you take things further. They should be able at least to point you in the right direction.

- Find a church that teaches the Bible well, runs introductory courses on the Bible or Christianity, and is friendly to sceptics and inquirers. Many of us live reasonably close to at least one church like this, and they usually have decent websites, so have a look and make a few inquiries. One way to find a church is through the Christianity Explored website: www.christianityexplored.org/findacourse

- I would certainly recommend reading one of the four Gospels found in the New Testament. For most people, I would recommend starting with the Gospel of Luke. If you don't have a Bible, you can read it online or have it read to you via a number of audio-book options. It's not that long—less than 20,000 words, which is far shorter than most novels. (By comparison, the first and shortest Harry Potter book has around 77,000 words!) It may seem strange in parts, and you might find it a little hard going, but don't worry. Just jot down any notes or questions you have and then ask a Christian friend about them. That's what I did.

Wherever you're at on the journey of life, I hope I've given you more than enough reason to (re)consider Christianity. I hope you see that it is intellectually sustainable and you are willing to investigate it further. But more than that: I hope that you will put your faith in Jesus and want to commit your life to him.

Acknowledgements

I would like to thank those who have given me great support and encouragement in writing this book.

The good folk (crew) of the Boathouse Church, Putney, London. Niel and Jana du Preez and George and Kimberley Johnston.

Those who helped with all my edits and many typos: Lucy Eastcott (the comma queen), Louise Stileman and Jo Shaw.

A special thanks to my wife Karen.

Endnotes

1 Shige Abe, "The Meaning of Life", Nasa Astrobiology Institute, https://astrobiology.nasa.gov/nai/articles/2001/7/6/the-meaning-of-life/index.html (accessed 18 March 2020).

2 C. Brown, "America's Passion for Jesus", *Reviews in American History* 32(3) (2004), p 439-446. Retrieved September 26, 2020, from http://www.jstor.org/stable/30031427.

3 Richard Dawkins, *The God Delusion* (10th Anniversary Edition, Black Swan, 2016), p 122.

4 G.A. Wells' article in "Jesus, Historicity of" in Tom Flynn, *The New Encyclopaedia of Unbelief* (Prometheus Books, 2007), p 446 onwards.

5 Tacitus, *Annals 1.11, Dio Cassius* 53.30.2. For further reading on both the Augustinian census and the dates of Quirinius' governorship, see the excellent excursus in Darrel Bock's first volume of his commentary on Luke's Gospel. Luke 1:1-9:50, Excursus 2, p 903-909.

6 Survey by Career Builder, http://press.careerbuilder.com/2014-08-07-Fifty-eight-Percent-of-Employers-Have-Caught-a-Lie-on-a-Resume-According-to-a-New-CareerBuilder-Survey (accessed 1 November 2019).

7 https://www.independent.co.uk/life-style/love-sex/are-we-meant-be-monogamous-why-people-cheat-open-relationships-and-life-after-affair-10097811.html (accessed 14 January 2021).

8 The quote is often attributed to Oswald J. Smith or Blaise Pascal

9 https://womenandhollywood.com/bette-gordon-talks-recognizing-the-evil-within-ourselves-in-the-drowning-e569d35d0310/ (accessed 05 November 2020).

10 Mark Twain, *Following the Equator: A Journey Around the World* (American Publishing Company, 1897), Chapter LXVI, Kindle Edition, Location 7101.

11 Clayborne Carson (ed), *The Autobiography of Martin Luther King, Jr.* (Intellectual Properties Management, Inc, 1998), p 357-358.

12 As quoted in https://www.express.co.uk/news/weird/11694 04/bible-news-jesus-fake-christianity-atheist-richard-dawkins-god-real-life-after-death-spt (accessed 1 February 2020).

13 C.S. Lewis, *Mere Christianity* (Collins, 1952), pp. 54–56.

14 Michka Assayas, *Bono on Bono: Conversations with Michka Assayas* (Hodder & Stoughton, 2005), p 204

15 Zealots were notoriously opposed to the Roman rule of their day and took up arms against the Romans. Many of them were nicknamed *sicarii* after the small daggers that they owned and used. Numerous scholars have argued that they were basically ancient terrorists involved in guerrilla warfare. It is highly likely that Barabbas was in prison for murdering a Roman soldier or worse, or at least for instigating violence..

16 To date, the book is yet to be translated into English.

17 C.S. Lewis, *Miracles* (William Collins, 1947), p 236-237.

18 See the Introduction to *Plutarch's The Life of Alexander* by Victor Davis Hanson (The Modern Library New York, 2004), especially p 12-14.

19 There is, in fact, so much Jewish scholarship on the resurrection of Jesus that a book has been written about it:

Jewish Scholarship on the Resurrection of Jesus by David Mishkin (Pickwick Publications, 2017).

20 E.P. Sanders, *The Historical Figure of Jesus* (Penguin, 1993), p 280.

21 N.T. Wright, *The Resurrection of the Son of God* (SPCK, 2003), p 718.

22 Robin Lane Fox, *The Classical World: An Epic History of Greece and Rome* (Penguin, 2005), p 534.

23 Paula Frederickson's remark was made during a discussion in the "Historical Jesus" section of the annual meeting of the Society of Biblical Literature, 22 November 1999. As quoted at https://www.reasonablefaith.org/writings/popular-writings/christianity-other-faiths/who-is-the-real-jesus-the-jesus-of-the-bible-or-the-jesus-of-the-quran/ (accessed 1 April 2020).

24 Paul Barnett, *The Truth About Jesus: The Challenge of the Evidence* (Aquila Press, 2000), p 131.

25 Barnett, p 115. Likewise N.T Wright states, "There is no evidence for a form of early Christianity in which the resurrection was not a central belief" (*The Challenge of Jesus* [Inter Varsity Press, 1999], p 133).

26 Senaca, *Epistulae Morales (Moral Letters)*, 101.14.

27 Tom Anderson, former president of the California Trial Lawyers Association. As quoted in Josh McDowell, *The Resurrection Factor* (Here's Life Publishers, 1981), p 66 (emphasis added).

thegoodbook
COMPANY

Thanks for reading this book. We hope you enjoyed it, and found it helpful.

Most people want to find answers to the big questions of life: Who are we? Why are we here? How should we live? But for many valid reasons we are often unable to find the time or the right space to think positively and carefully about them.

Perhaps you have questions that you need an answer for. Perhaps you have met Christians who have seemed unsympathetic or incomprehensible. Or maybe you are someone who has grown up believing, but need help to make things a little clearer.

At The Good Book Company, we're passionate about producing materials that help people of all ages and stages understand the heart of the Christian message, which is found in the pages of the Bible.

Whoever you are, and wherever you are at when it comes to these big questions, we hope we can help. As a publisher we want to help you look at the good book that is the Bible because we're convinced that as we meet the person who stands at its heart—Jesus Christ—we find the clearest answers to our biggest questions.

Visit our website to discover the range of books, videos and other resources we produce, or visit our partner site www.christianityexplored.org for a clear explanation of who Jesus is and why he came.

Thanks again for reading,

Your friends at The Good Book Company

thegoodbook.com | thegoodbook.co.uk
thegoodbook.com.au | thegoodbook.co.nz | thegoodbook.co.in

WWW.CHRISTIANITYEXPLORED.ORG

Our partner site is a great place to explore the Christian faith, with powerful testimonies and answers to difficult questions.